DAD, WHAT'S FOR DINNER?

Alfred A. Knopf
New York
2025

DAD, WHAT'S FOR DINNER?

Lifesaving Recipes to Avoid Meltdowns, Have Fun in the Kitchen, and Keep Your Kids Well Fed

DAVID NAYFELD

with Joshua David Stein

Photography by Eric Wolfinger
Foreword by Gwyneth Paltrow

THIS IS A BORZOI BOOK
PUBLISHED BY ALFRED A. KNOPF

Text copyright © 2025 by The Nayfeld Family Trust
Photographs copyright © 2025 by Eric Wolfinger
Foreword copyright © 2025 by Gwyneth Paltrow

aaknopf.com

Knopf, Borzoi Books, and the colophon are registered trademarks of Penguin Random House LLC.

Library of Congress Cataloging-in-Publication Data

Names: Nayfeld, David, author. | Stein, Joshua David, author. |
    Wolfinger, Eric, photographer.
Title: Dad, what's for dinner? / David Nayfeld with Joshua David Stein ; photography by Eric Wolfinger.
Description: First edition. | New York : Alfred A. Knopf, 2025. | Includes index.
Identifiers: LCCN 2024019017 (print) | LCCN 2024019018 (ebook) |
    ISBN 9780593537527 (hardcover) | ISBN 9780593537534 (ebook)
Subjects: LCSH: Cooking. | Cooking for children. | LCGFT: Cookbooks.
Classification: LCC TX714 .N39 2025 (print) | LCC TX714 (ebook) |
    DDC 641.5/622--dc23/eng/20240517
LC record available at https://lccn.loc.gov/2024019017
LC ebook record available at https://lccn.loc.gov/2024019018

Some of the recipes in this book may include raw eggs, meat, or fish. When these foods are consumed raw, there is always the risk that bacteria, which is killed by proper cooking, may be present. For this reason, when serving these foods raw, always buy certified salmonella-free eggs and the freshest meat and fish available from a reliable grocer, storing them in the refrigerator until they are served. Because of the health risks associated with the consumption of bacteria that can be present in raw eggs, meat, and fish, these foods should not be consumed by infants, small children, pregnant women, the elderly, or any persons who may be immunocompromised. The author and publisher expressly disclaim responsibility for any adverse effects that may result from the use or application of the recipes and information contained in this book.

Cover photographs by Eric Wolfinger
Cover design by Ashley Tucker

Manufactured in China
First Edition

To Helena: Your world will
be as big as you imagine
it to be. I love you.
—David Nayfeld (Dad)

For my sons and mother.
—JDS

CONTENTS

Meat/Fish/Poultry 124

Salads 178

Veggies 190

Bread and Things on It 222

Snacks/Sweets 252

Resources 288

FOREWORD

My dad was so many things to me: a supreme gourmand who taught me what it meant to appreciate good food, the most nurturing man I've ever known, and the maker of the world's best pancake. I still feel close to him every time I step into the kitchen. Or taste something, really, really good—a meal so exceptional the experience is somatic, best communicated through sounds that never quite take the form of words. The pursuit of that feeling has brought me evermore deeply into my own kitchen, a journey I explored in my first cookbook *My Father's Daughter,* and it has taken me to so many incredible restaurants over the years. It is in these kitchens that I've inadvertently forged friendships that continue to enrich my life.

David Nayfeld is one of these friends. We first met in San Francisco, in 2018, when I had the great privilege of devouring one of Che Fico's famous sourdough pizzas. I remember it living up to the hype. And I remember how I felt after: better than I normally feel after eating a full pizza. Maybe that was due to the dough's long fermentation process. Or maybe it was an outcome of the environment, a space warmed by David's kindness and the generous spirit he created for everyone in it. David's perfectionism and obsession with deliciousness resonated with me deeply. We quickly bonded and became friends. Over the years I have watched his entrepreneurial spirit fully take flight. He has opened restaurants. He has created his own value set and instilled it in his teams. And most importantly, he has become a single dad, raising a daughter with dedication and commitment.

This cookbook is a love letter to, in my biased view, the most epic of all love stories: the love between a father and his daughter. Yes, in its pages you will find gorgeous, flavor-filled recipes that work. You will find ways to make restaurant-quality meals at home. You will learn tips and tricks that will make you a better cook. But most importantly, you will do so within the framework of the kind of love that reminds you what life is all about. That being fully present in the kitchen with someone you adore, and making meals with or for them, makes the world slow down and feel a lot cozier.

—Gwyneth Paltrow

DAD, WHAT'S FOR DINNER?

I am a professional chef. I've spent twenty-seven of my forty years in some of the best kitchens in the world: Eleven Madison Park in New York, Joël Robuchon in Las Vegas, and Aqua in San Francisco. In 2018, I opened my first restaurant, a high-ceilinged homage to the Italian food I loved in an old auto body shop on Divisadero in downtown San Francisco. We strung herbs from the ceiling, installed a pizza oven, started our own charcuterie and pasta program, and called the restaurant Che Fico! (*che fico!* translates to "cool!"). Though I had been trained in fine dining, I wanted my own project to be a place where people could gather to relax, enjoy our handmade pastas, pizzas, salads, secondi, and lots of wine. The focus was on lusty flavors and high-quality ingredients. The beauty was that you felt like family. Che Fico! was named Best New Restaurant by *Esquire* when it opened and has gained a devoted following. The year after I opened Che Fico Alimentari just downstairs, followed by Che Fico Parco Menlo (in Menlo Park) and Che Fico Mercato, a market also in Menlo Park. So, I'm used to professional kitchens, high-pressure environments where everything is measured in seconds and centimeters.

And still, when my daughter, Helena, asks, "Dad, what's for dinner?" it gets me every time.

This book, and the recipes it contains, are born of the fact that neither "nothing" nor "I don't know" is an acceptable answer. Dinner *has* to get on the table.

Think of this as a guide, as a resource, really, as a friendly helping hand. I want it to help you answer the question of what's for dinner—and what's for breakfast, and what's for lunch; a response to every *Daddy, I'm hungry. I need a snack.* But just as important to me as the eighty recipes, I want to give you the tools and techniques you need to create a functional home kitchen so that you can feed your family.

Everything here is written from a specific point of view, *my* point of view, as a father and as a chef. Some of these recipes were born even before Helena was. They hail from years of eating, and preparing so-called family meals, when restaurant staff gather to be fed before service. There I learned the importance of both thrift and haste. A family meal has to be delicious, it has to be cheap, and it has to be easy enough to cram into the time between finishing prepping your station and before service. (You can tell a lot about a chef by how much effort they devote to their family meal. It's what shows you for whom cooking is just a job and for whom it is a calling.)

What better training for being a parent? For these principles are even more salient when you're talking not about your restaurant family but your family family. Add to that, immeasurable love, the kind you feel for your kids but probably not your coworkers, the kind that makes you want to cook them the most delicious food you possibly can; the fact that your kids are kids and their palates are both different and your responsibility to develop; the idea that your time is limited with them—they grow up so fast!—and cooking can be an important joint activity, and you'll begin to see where my head is at when I developed these recipes. To be clear, this isn't "kid food." It's important to me that I raise adventurous and confident kids. A lot of that starts with what they eat. And since naturally what they eat depends on what you can make, throughout this book I also introduce you to the valuable systems I use to keep my family fed.

This isn't a book just for fathers, or single fathers, or mothers or single mothers or grandparents, aunts and uncles, or older sisters and brothers. It's a book for anyone who cares about another person and wants to do that thing that shows they care: cook. It is, however, a book that I wrote and I am a single father, with a daughter, Helena, whom I care about and whom I cook for and whom I love very much.

Helena is an entire constellation of bright shining light compressed into a five-year-old child. She's tenacious and sweet and wonderful and, being a kid, depends on me for every meal. It was Helena who gave me the title for this book because *Dad, what's for dinner?* is her single most often asked question. It's a question that now fills me with a deep sense of joy, the same joy I feel when I extend my hand down and her tiny fingers grasp mine. But it can be a daunting one.

The reason I want to share my story isn't because this is my book or because I think it's extraordinary. I want to share it precisely because it isn't. In fact, a lot of fathers—a lot of parents—have similar experiences, but we all feel so boxed in by shame, or maybe a natural aversion to sharing the less-than-rosy details of our lives, that the stories don't get told. The result is just more shame and more isolation. The anxiety that we're not living up to the ideal of parenthood festers. Because the motivating spirit of this book is honesty—honesty in recipes, honesty in headnotes, honesty everywhere. I'm going to start now.

Helena was born in 2019. I was never married to her mother, and we split up two and a half years later. The breakup was, and continues to be, highly adversarial. For six months, I could see Helena only in two-hour increments, every Tuesday and Thursday. I lived an hour away, so we'd play together in a park or go to a coffee shop. She couldn't understand why she couldn't come home with Daddy. It was one of the hardest points in my life. It was, and I know many parents can relate, humiliating and demoralizing. I relied on those four hours with her as a reason to keep going.

The one thing I had in my arsenal that I knew I could do was cook. I would prepare big batches of rigatoni in vodka sauce, pasta with ragu Bolognese or Genovese, chicken soup, sausage and kale soup, things I knew would travel well in the car and that she could eat from one container with minimal mess. I'd pack three bags: one with toys and crafts; another with clothes, diapers, and sunscreen; and another full of thermoses, lunch boxes, Tupperware with food. Often my mom, Baba Galina, would come with me because it was the only time she got to see her grandchild. I could see how sad she felt for me. Later she told me how proud she was that I wasn't willing to stop trying.

When Helena turned three, she finally started spending the night at my house. The thought of cooking alone in the kitchen when she was in another room playing seemed like such a waste. So we cooked together. These are some of my favorite memories: her standing next to me making "cuppycakes," or helping me roll out pasta. Never has "Dad, what's for dinner?" felt more like a privilege. The more I cooked, the more I realized that the expertise I had gained from working in restaurants was applicable at home, too. The same principles that underpin a successful kitchen—organization, resourcefulness, efficiency—don't stop as soon as you leave work. But what I also learned firsthand was that the more I could involve Helena in the cooking, the easier it was to get her to eat the food.

Over time, my family grew. I met a radiant woman named Vanessa, now my fiancée. Now her teenage son, Niko, lives with us. So there are more mouths to feed and less time to do so. Helena, too, though never a wallflower, has developed her own voice and her own tastes. She lets me know when she's not a fan of my food. And yet, I feel more confident that I can manage, more confident that I can answer "Dad, what's for dinner?" with a response that is both satisfying and realistic.

I hope this book, and these recipes, which constitute the lessons I've learned as a father cooking for his family, will help you answer that question, too. They're full of tips and tricks and suggestions for how you, too, can have your kid help you. None of these recipes are meant to be inviolable. If you want to modify them, go ahead. I won't be mad. They're here for you, answers for what's for dinner and reminders that in this slogging, joyful, stressful, wondrous project of parenting, you're not alone.

ON YIELD

Most of these recipes are designed for four people, with some leftovers. It's a nice round number. I've included instructions for storage, reuse, and leftovers. At my house, and at yours, nothing should go to waste.

ON TIME

More than space, more than money, time often feels like the most precious commodity. After a long day of work—or before a long day of work—crammed between chores, homework, ideally some sort of unstructured bonding, bedtime, fighting about bedtime, really serious this time bedtime, the idea that you'd have time to prepare a freshly made meal seems absurdly optimistic. I get it. I live that. The majority of these recipes take 45 minutes or less to prepare. When they take more time, most of it is hands-off (e.g., a soup simmers, a meat braises, a cake bakes). Some recipes, though, take longer. I reserve these for when either I'm cooking *with* my family (so the cooking is an activity) or to make in whatever stretch of time I have alone. Keeping in mind how costly time is, I've made sure to accurately calculate how much is needed for each recipe. I've also categorized each recipe in a way that makes sense to me (and I think will make sense to most parents):

Meals that can be made in 30 minutes or less. For when you just need to get something on the table.

Meals that can be made in 30 to 60 minutes. You've had some time to plan ahead and are not insanely stressed.

More involved meals, perfect for weekends, when you have days off, and when you want to cook with your kid. These can take an hour or more.

ON MESS

The kitchen adage "clean as you go" has never been more important than when bedtime (plus prebedtime meltdowns and postbedtime story time) lurks on the far side of dinner. I've tried as best I can to minimize the amount of equipment used as well as the mess generated. This isn't to say the more pans the more mess necessarily. (Some pans take just a quick swipe; some demand thankless scrubbing.) For each recipe, I've rated the mess from 1 (minimal) to 4 (substantial). No matter the rating, try as best you can to clean each vessel as you go.

Tip: Be relentless in cleaning as you go. When I have even 60 seconds of downtime while I'm cooking, I am cleaning a pan or a whisk or putting things away. By the time dinner is on the table, the kitchen—save for the serving vessel, plates, and cutlery—is cleaned. This completely changes the game.

Also, if you've just come back from the grocery store, use the grocery bag as your garbage bag. Place it right next to the work area.

Cooking with Your Kids
vs. Cooking for Your Kids
AN IMPORTANT DISTINCTION

Sometimes you want to cook with your kids and your kids want to cook with you. That's great. I love that. It's the ideal. But realistically, sometimes you have 30 minutes or less to get something on the table and it just isn't the time for collaboration. Or maybe you have the time but it's tantrum o'clock or homework needs to get done or one thousand other small factors that form the friction of fatherhood get in the way. Knowing when to chase the ideal and when to embrace the reality is also part, a very important part, of being a dad.

Generally in this book, projects that are perfect for your kids to help with are those that take more time, the Project Cooking recipes. Sheeting out pasta, for example, or making ravioli or baking cookies (baking is kid-helping central). But even those recipes that don't, at first glance, seem like an opportunity to get your kid in the kitchen can be a chance to work together. I'm allergic to aspirational parenting pablum, so I'll just say, do what's right for you and your family. You know your kid best. You know yourself best. I, for instance, am not going to stop Helena, even if she is doing a potentially dangerous activity, like stirring a hot pot, if she is executing it with focus and observing correct protocol. If she is to get hurt, I'd rather

she does so in my care, so I can help her. That's why I
divided the following tasks up by level, not by age. Think
of it like a car wash. Each level up includes all services
from the lower levels. But don't worry. You don't have to
memorize this. Throughout the book, I've called out specific steps that kids can help with.

LEVEL I

Zero risk, except a mess.

- Measuring out ingredients and adding to bowls
- Picking herbs
- Cutting with safe kid-friendly knives
- Stirring nonheated ingredients in bowls
- Seasoning off the heat, with premeasured spices
- Rolling out dough
- Breaking eggs

LEVEL II

A little bit of risk, a little bit of skill.

- Adding ingredients to a moving mixer
- Forming and shaping things like meatballs and cookies
- Seasoning off the heat, with supervision
- Stirring with a wooden spoon or spatula on the stove

LEVEL III

Now we're cooking.

- Using sharp knives
- Turning the stove on
- Adding ingredients to hot pans
- Removing the pans from the stove
- Transferring ingredients from hot pans
- Being able to fully lead a project without parental supervision

BREAKFA

ST

NO OTHER MEAL IN THE DAY IS AS TRANSFORMED BY
the school calendar as breakfast. During the academic year, weekday
breakfasts fall into the "Hurry up and eat, so we can get out the door"
camp. Breakfast is you get what you get. If it's a piece of fruit and a piece
of toast on the way out the door, consider yourself lucky. My mother
would warm six mozzarella sticks in the toaster oven. I ate that every
morning for two years.

But on weekends—and during breaks—breakfast can be a luxurious
and leisurely way to start a day. In fact, because it is normally so rushed,
I find those laid-back breakfasts to be the most joyful meal in the house.
And, because so much of breakfast is baking-centric, it's a great opportunity to bond with your kid. Or, let them relax and sleep in while you
make it. It doesn't matter. That's the great part about the weekend.

These recipes are mostly for those lazy mornings when small hands
can help and the clock can be ignored. But there's a few in here of the
weekday variety, too. These have been stress-tested over the past year in
my own home. From start to finish to getting the bowl out you should be
able to get them done in under 10 minutes.

MELTDOWN MEAL

PROTEIN-PACKED YOGURT PARFAIT WITH DUKKAH AND SEASONAL FRUIT

¾ cup (200g) plain whole-milk Greek yogurt

½ scoop (15g) protein powder

1 to 2 tablespoons milk (optional)

⅓ cup (40g) granola

½ cup (3 ounces/90g) fresh berries

½ banana, sliced

1½ teaspoons honey, preferably local

1 teaspoon dukkah (recipe follows)

Dukkah—which comes from the Arabic word ''to pound''—is an easy to make spice mix traditionally made with nuts, often hazelnuts, and a variety of herbs. Some families use mint, others sesame, za'atar, marjoram, and cumin. I keep it simple with coriander and fennel, though feel free to experiment yourself. Dukkah keeps up to a month in an airtight container so I usually make 2 cups and top yogurt with fruit with a scoop (as seen here) or sprinkle some on toast with peanut butter and apple (page 235). I find the condiment is a nice way to adultify kids' snacks (and ever so gently expand their palates).

In a bowl, stir together the yogurt and protein powder until well blended. If it looks too thick, add some milk. Add the granola, fruit, honey, and dukkah on top. Serve immediately.

Making a spice mix,
like dukkah, is an
excellent opportunity
to familiarize your
kid with the wonders
of your spice cabinet.
Go ahead, sniff around.

DUKKAH

YIELD: MAKES 1½ CUPS (212G)

TIME: 20 MINUTES

MESS: 1/4

¼ cup (30g) pistachios

¼ cup (35g) blanched almonds

¼ cup (35g) hazelnuts

¼ cup (25g) walnuts

¼ cup (35g) sunflower seeds

1 tablespoon coriander seeds

1 tablespoon fennel seeds

1 tablespoon (15g) coarse sea salt

1. Preheat the oven to 325°F (160°C).

2. In a bowl, stir together the nuts and the seeds. Spread evenly on a sheet pan and toast in the oven for 20 minutes. Remove and let cool completely.

3. Once cooled, place in a food processor and pulse. Add the salt and pulse again quickly.

SWEET OATMEAL

MELTDOWN
MEAL

4 cups (950ml) whole milk,
plus more for serving

Pinch of kosher salt

1 cup (200g) Irish steel-cut oats

1 tablespoon maple syrup

½ banana, sliced, for serving

A few strawberries, topped and
quartered, for serving

There's nothing fancy here. Even if I'm making
this for only two, I'll make a full recipe as
it reheats extremely well, just 2 or 3 minutes
in the microwave (or in a pan with a splash of
milk over medium heat; just break up the oatmeal
with a spatula or a wooden spoon). Often I'll
make one portion for Helena and one for me, that
I'll stash in a container to eat on the road for
those mornings — every morning — when we're running
behind.

1. In a saucepan, bring the milk and salt to a boil over medium-high heat, stirring occasionally, being careful not to scorch the milk. Add the oats. Reduce the heat to medium-low, cover, and cook, stirring occasionally, until the oats are tender, 15 to 20 minutes.

2. Stir in the maple syrup.

3. To serve, ladle into four bowls. Top with bananas, strawberries, and a splash of cold milk.

STRESSED-OUT WEEKDAY PANCAKES

1 ripe banana

1 tablespoon vanilla extract

1 teaspoon ground cinnamon

⅔ cup (160ml) whole milk

1 cup (120g) Bob's Red Mill
(or similar) Pancake and
Waffle Mix

2 tablespoons (30g) unsalted
butter, plus more for serving

Maple syrup, for serving

EQUIPMENT:

#10 (3-ounce) ice cream scoop

These easy-to-make and fluffy pancakes hold in them an essential lesson of fatherhood. One morning I was feeling triumphant. Helena was up and dressed. I was up and dressed. I made these pancakes and fed her every last bite, which she happily ate. As a single dad I felt I had no margin of error about getting her to school on time, or anything else. I was constantly proving myself. That day I could do no wrong. We drove the 45 minutes to school; all was golden. Then, just as we're getting out of the car, Helena looks at me and says, "I think I'm going to vom—" Before she can finish the sentence, she throws up over everything. My car. Her clothes. The car seat. The day quickly took a turn. Luckily, I had a go bag with me with an extra set of clothes. So, I quickly changed Helena, and she made it to school on time after all. The lesson? You're a hero. You're a loser. You're a hero again. That, to me, is what being a dad can be like.

As far as this recipe goes, I use Bob's Red Mill pancake mix because you don't need to add anything to it, but use whatever you have. If your mix calls for an egg, then add it. The tweak here is the addition of smashed banana, cinnamon, and vanilla, and for that I need to give credit to Vanessa, my fiancée, who pioneered the technique and makes the mornings infinitely less stressful.

Mornings are a grind, but multiple studies show that children who eat breakfast not only have increased brain function but also better learning outcomes.

1. In a bowl, mash the banana with a fork until it's smashed but still chunky. Add the vanilla, cinnamon, and milk and mix them together with the fork. Add the pancake mix to the bowl and incorporate with the fork until you achieve a shaggy batter.

2. Heat a well-seasoned stainless steel sauté pan or cast-iron or nonstick skillet over medium-high heat. Add 1 tablespoon of the butter to the hot pan. The butter should melt quickly but should not smoke. When the butter melts and the water in it evaporates, the butter will look clear and start to brown and smell nutty.

3. Use an ice cream scoop to add a baseball-sized amount of batter to the pan. Let the batter cook for 2 minutes, without touching it. The edges will start to brown on the bottom and small holes will start to appear in the center of the batter.

4. Use a pancake turner to carefully loosen the pancake from the bottom of the pan. Flip the pancake and cook it on the other side for an additional 2 minutes. Repeat with the remaining batter.

5. Remove the pancake from the pan and serve immediately with butter and maple syrup.

LAZY WEEKEND PANCAKES

WEEKNIGHT MEAL

2 cups (320g) whole wheat flour (stone-milled, if available)

¼ cup (50g) raw sugar

2 teaspoons (6g) baking powder

1 teaspoon (5g) baking soda

1 teaspoon (3g) kosher salt

2 large eggs (60g each), separated

1½ cups (350g) buttermilk

1 cup (245g) whole milk

2 tablespoons (30g) distilled white vinegar

1 tablespoon (15g) vanilla extract

4 tablespoons (55g) unsalted butter, melted and cooled

TO FINISH:

4 tablespoons (55g) unsalted butter, plus more for serving

Maple syrup, for serving

EQUIPMENT:

Electric mixer

For anyone who has not gone through the exercise of making a true pancake from scratch, know there are few things more satisfying. The level of primal urge satisfaction is akin to being a hunter, killing your own venison and bringing it back to the table. Actually, making pancakes from scratch isn't that hard. The secret—and the science experiment—is that the vinegar reacts with the baking soda to form a foamy texture. The most time-consuming part of this recipe is the measuring out of ingredients—but what might be tedious for you is fun for your kids, so get them involved. And a word about texture: Some people like soft, singularly textured pancakes. I do not. By cooking them at a higher heat, you achieve a crisp crust that yields to a tender fluffy interior. Nothing could be better.

1. In a bowl, stir together the flour, sugar, baking powder, baking soda, and salt.

2. In a second bowl, with an electric mixer, whip the egg whites until they create soft peaks.

3. In a third bowl, whisk together the egg yolks, buttermilk, milk, vinegar, vanilla, and 4 tablespoons melted butter.

4. Stir the buttermilk mixture into the flour mixture with a rubber spatula, stirring just until combined. Be careful not to overmix. Fold in the egg whites.

RECIPE CONTINUES

5. Melt 1 tablespoon of the butter in a stainless steel skillet over high heat. Once melted, reduce the heat to medium and scoop ½-cup (120ml) portions of batter into the hot pan. Cook until the edges become crispy and bubbles start to appear on the surface of the pancake, 1 to 2 minutes. Flip and continue to cook until the edges are crispy and the center is firm. Repeat with the rest of the batter.

6. Serve with butter and maple syrup.

There's a lot of measuring here. Enlist your
kids as measurers- and mixers-in-chief.

JOINT CUSTARDY FRENCH TOAST

1 loaf challah, cut into thick slabs
(2 to 2½ inches/5 to 6.5cm)

5 large eggs

1 pint (470ml) heavy cream

1½ teaspoons ground cinnamon

1 tablespoon vanilla extract

½ teaspoon ground ginger
(optional)

2 tablespoons maple syrup,
plus more for serving

Pinch of kosher salt

8 tablespoons (4 ounces/115g)
unsalted butter, plus more for
serving

Coarse sea salt, for serving

This is not a last-minute breakfast. This is a
pièce de résistance breakfast, a two-or-three-
times-a-year breakfast, an ''I need to hit it out
of the park'' breakfast. To make really good French
toast takes some foresight, since the key is
allowing the challah—cut much thicker than normal
here—to get stale for a full day and then letting
it soak in the custard mixture much longer than you
think it should. (Never have 10 minutes passed so
slowly.) But the result is that what emerges from
the oven is challah on the outside and custard on
the inside. It might be the most delicious bite
Hashem has ever created.

1. One day out, place the cut challah on a wire rack and set
it out to dry overnight.

2. When ready to cook the French toast, preheat the oven to
375°F (190°C). Line a sheet pan with a wire rack. Set aside.

3. In a bowl, whisk together the eggs, cream, cinnamon,
vanilla, ginger (if using), maple syrup, and salt until smooth.
Pour into a large shallow baking dish.

4. Lay the challah slices in the custard to soak for 10 minutes.
Don't crowd the challah. Leave some space between the
pieces for the custard to properly work its magic. Flip over
and soak for another 10 minutes. If the slices are not totally
saturated, continue to soak until they are.

RECIPE CONTINUES

5. Heat a sauté pan over medium-high heat. Melt ½ tablespoon butter, allowing it to get foamy. Reduce the heat to medium, add a slice of French toast, and cook without disturbing it for about 2 minutes. Flip the French toast to the other side and cook for an additional 2 minutes. Place the finished French toast on the wire rack in the sheet pan.

6. Repeat with the rest of the slices, adding 2 tablespoons of butter to the pan after every 2 slices (or as needed). Pay attention to the color—you want toasted, deeply golden brown—and don't be afraid to adjust the heat as needed.

7. Once all the French toast is done, slide the sheet pan into the oven and bake until hot in the center, 7 to 10 minutes.

8. To serve, spread butter on the top of each piece to taste. Drizzle maple syrup and sprinkle coarse sea salt on top.

BISCUITS WITH SAUSAGE AND PEPPER GRAVY

FOR THE BISCUITS:

3 cups (425g) all-purpose or whole wheat pastry (preferred) flour, plus more for dusting

2 tablespoons (20g) baking powder

½ teaspoon (2g) baking soda

1½ teaspoons (5g) kosher salt

12 tablespoons (6 ounces/170g) unsalted butter, cut into ½-inch (13mm) cubes, frozen

1¼ cups (300g) buttermilk, plus more for brushing

8 ounces (225g) sharp cheddar cheese, grated

Coarse sea salt

FOR THE COUNTRY GRAVY:

6 tablespoons (3 ounces/85g) unsalted butter

1 cup (150g) finely diced yellow onion

5 garlic cloves, minced

2 pounds (910g) bulk breakfast sausage

2 tablespoons all-purpose flour

2 cups (470ml) buttermilk

½ cup (120ml) pepper brine (from a jar of banana peppers)

My love affair with biscuits began, like most people's who do not live in the South, at KFC. When I was a boy, my Belarussian grandmother, Fira, would walk me across Alameda to KFC for tangy BBQ strips of chicken, a side of mashed potatoes, and a biscuit. That flaky buttery biscuit is what I've tried to re-create here, augmented by a *lot* of cheddar and honey. As for the gravy, it's rich. It's sweet. No one who tries it isn't won over.

1. Make the biscuits: Preheat the oven to 425°F (220°C). Line a sheet pan with parchment paper.

2. In a bowl, stir together the flour, baking powder, baking soda, and salt and refrigerate until chilled.

3. In a food processor, combine the frozen butter cubes and chilled flour mixture. Pulse several times until the butter is pea-sized. Add the buttermilk and cheddar and quick-mix until the dough looks shaggy, being careful not to overmix.

4. Dust a work surface lightly with flour and turn the dough out onto it. Quickly bring the dough together with your hands (it should be cold to the touch). Roll with a floured rolling pin into

Kneading and rolling out dough and, most especially, punching out the biscuits, is kid-help central.

RECIPE AND INGREDIENTS CONTINUE

Grated zest and juice of 1 large lemon

1 tablespoon Dijon mustard

1 teaspoon Calabrian chili bomba (see page 293)

1 (12-ounce/340g) jar sweet banana peppers (or pepperoncini), cut into rings

½ cup (100g) sour cream

Kosher salt and freshly ground black pepper

Sliced green onions, for garnish

a rough rectangle. With a long side of the rectangle facing you, fold in thirds by bringing the two short ends in toward the center. Roll out again until 1 inch (2.5cm) thick. Fold in thirds again, widthwise, making sure the middle creases come together. Roll gently once more and create a 6½-inch (16.5cm) square. Cut into 9 biscuits (3 across, 3 down). Place on the parchment-lined pan and chill in the refrigerator for 15 minutes.

5. Brush the biscuits with buttermilk and sprinkle coarse sea salt on top.

6. Bake until a dark golden brown, 20 to 22 minutes.

7. Let sit in the pan on the rack for 5 minutes before serving.

NOTE: *I like to keep a couple of sticks of butter, cut into cubes, in the freezer. That way, when making pie crusts or biscuits, you're ready to go.*

8. **Make the country gravy:** In a wide shallow pot or rondeau, melt 4 tablespoons (55g) of the butter over medium-high heat. Add the onion and sauté for 1 to 2 minutes. Add the garlic and sauté until fragrant, 1 to 2 minutes.

9. Add the sausage, breaking it up with a wooden spoon, and cook until dark golden brown. The sausage pieces should be about dime-sized. Remove with a slotted spoon and set aside on a plate.

10. In the same pot, melt the remaining 2 tablespoons (30g) butter. Whisk in the flour and stir constantly until the roux turns light brown, about 3 to 5 minutes. Add the buttermilk, whisking constantly and scraping the bits from the bottom and sides of the pot, to incorporate more flavor and to prevent scorching.

11. Once the gravy has thickened (it should be able to coat the back of a spoon), add the pepper brine, lemon zest, lemon juice, mustard, and chili bomba. Stir until combined. Add the banana peppers.

12. Remove from the heat. Stir in the sour cream until combined. Add salt and pepper to taste.

13. To serve, spoon the gravy over the hot biscuits. Garnish with green onions.

BATCH-

COOKING

WHEN IT COMES TO COOKING FOR KIDS, THE SINGLE biggest game changer for me was realizing the power of batch-cooking or, as we call it in restaurants, cooking. Restaurant chefs have a hard time cooking for two people. If I'm going to go to the effort of making stock, I'm going to make 12 quarts, not 2, since it's the same amount of work. But restaurants have walk-in refrigerators and scores of people eating there every night. Homes do not.

When Helena was born, I quickly realized a civilian fridge is a very different beast than a capacious restaurant walk-in. Helena, her mother, and I, plus Cassidy, my 90-pound pit bull, were living in a tiny one-bedroom apartment in San Francisco. Rather quickly, all my kitchen projects disappeared—the misos, the pickles, the collection of fancy amari—and gave way to bottles of milk and more bottles of milk. The freezer, and being efficient about filling it, became clutch.

And I was nearly as tight on time as I was on space. Helena filled my entire day. Between my work, her breakfast, naps, music class, park visits, more naps, maybe twenty minutes to build a fort and maybe two minutes for *me* to take a nap, I'd have to prep lunch and dinner. Now that she's older and in school—an hour away—the crunch hasn't stopped.

Given all that, batch-cooking makes a whole lot of sense. Instead of cooking for many people at once, however, I'm cooking for a few people over time. Helena loves ragu, for instance, but there's no way I'm spending 3½ hours every week to make it. A whole beef shank is enough to feed our family four times. One batch can last for months.

The secret to batch-cooking (and soup making) and your way into the parenting hall of fame is a $60 piece of equipment called a vacuum sealer. (I use a brand called FoodSaver.) I know, it's extra equipment. But it's pretty compact and a true lifesaver. Years of cooking in restaurants have convinced me of the value of vacuum sealing. It both saves space and elongates the lifespan of food—even if you aren't freezing it. But I *do* freeze it. After I make a batch of whatever it is—stocks, soups, sauces—I'll let it cool. Then I divide it into about 1,000-gram portions, enough for four to six people—many vacuum sealers come with cut-to-order bags, so cut what makes sense for your family—fill as many bags as I can, lay them flat, label them with the date, and freeze them, almost like filling a filing cabinet. When I'm in need of a quick dinner, I run a bag under hot water until it's thawed—and, in 15 minutes, a delicious meal is on the table.

CHICKEN STOCK

1 whole chicken (3 pounds/1.4kg)

2 pounds (910g) chicken wings

3 large carrots, peeled and cut into large pieces

4 celery stalks, cut into large pieces

1 pound (450g) large yellow onions, cut into large pieces

1 bunch fresh parsley stems (optional)

1 head garlic, halved horizontally

10 sprigs fresh thyme

3 fresh bay leaves (optional)

EQUIPMENT:

FoodSaver (optional) or ziplock bags with the air removed

Ideal for when your kids are out (or asleep) and you have some free time. (Meaning, your kids will appreciate this, but it might not be the recipe they help with.)

Stock has kind of a mystique around it, because stock makes everything richer and more flavorful. On the other hand, though, stock is really just heavily fortified water. So if you can make tea, you can make stock. What you're doing is allowing the boiling water to leach out all the collagen—fat and flavor—from the bones and then adding a bunch of aromatics. That's it. Time and heat do the work; you don't. This recipe makes a perfect all-purpose stock for soups and sauces, or if you're going to deglaze a pan for a pan sauce. But if you want, you can let it simmer even longer than an hour, until the collagen becomes more concentrated. That concentrated stock, with some fresh ginger and lemon, is perfect for sipping to fend off colds and the flu.

1. Wash the chicken and chicken wings in scalding hot water under a faucet for 2 minutes. Remove any stray feathers and schmutz, place the chicken and wings in a large stockpot, and cover with enough cold water to submerge by 2 inches (5cm).

2. Bring the liquid to a lively simmer over high heat, adjusting the heat as needed to ensure that it doesn't start boiling. Skim any foam on the surface with a slotted spoon and let simmer for 45 minutes. Remove the whole chicken with tongs and place in a bowl.

STORAGE: Allow the stock to cool, then vacuum-seal in 2-cup (500ml) portions and freeze.

USE CHICKEN STOCK FOR:

Chicken Enchilada Stew (page 62)

Immunity Soup (page 70)

Jewish Mother's Chicken Soup (page 67)

Shepherd's Pie (page 175)

Stracciatella (page 55)

Tuscan Sausage, Bean, and Kale Soup (page 56)

3. Add the carrots, celery, onion, parsley stems (if using), garlic, thyme, and bay leaves (if using) and simmer for 25 minutes.

4. Meanwhile, when the chicken is cool enough to handle, pick the meat off the bones and from the wings. Discard the skin and return the bones to the pot. (Reserve the meat for later use, such as Jewish Mother's Chicken Soup, page 67.)

5. Continue to simmer the stock for 1 hour. Strain through a fine-mesh sieve into a bowl.

BEEF STOCK

6½ pounds (2.95kg) beef marrow bones, knuckle bones, or any other combination of collagen-rich bones

2 large carrots, cut into large pieces

1 yellow onion, halved

2 celery stalks, cut into large pieces

½ head garlic, halved horizontally

EQUIPMENT:

FoodSaver (optional) or ziplock bags with the air removed

Collagen helps kids develop strong bones and strengthens their immune systems.

In any recipe that calls for chicken stock, you can use beef stock for, too. It tends to have a richer flavor and texture, which is from the higher levels of collagen. Beef stock also makes a wonderful sipping broth for cold winter nights (recipe follows). Basically, for this and the chicken stock (and everything in this book and in life, too), the idea is not to waste what you have. If, for instance, you make Ragu Genovese (page 41), you'll have a big tibia bone. Use that. If you are making short ribs, use those, or a bone-in rib eye. The idea is to just submerge the bones. And if the water evaporates, you know what to do. (If you don't know what to do, the answer is to add more water.)

Used-up beef and pork bones are great doggie treats!

1. Preheat the oven to 400°F (200°C). Line a sheet pan with aluminum foil.

2. Spread the bones evenly over the pan. Roast the bones until golden brown, 45 to 50 minutes.

3. Remove the bones from the oven and transfer to a large stockpot. Scrape as much fat off the sheet pan as possible and transfer to the pot as well. Add the carrots, onion, celery, and garlic. Add water to cover the bones by 1 inch (2.5cm). Heat the stockpot over high heat, then allow to simmer uncovered for 1½ hours.

4. Add another 1 quart (1L) water and simmer for an additional hour. Remove from the heat and let the broth sit for 30 minutes.

USE BEEF STOCK FOR:

Shepherd's Pie (page 175)

Sipping Broth (at right)

Stracciatella (page 55)

Turkey Chili (page 65)

Tuscan Sausage, Bean, and Kale Soup (page 56)

A NOTE ABOUT STOCK IN GENERAL: *Geez Louise. Can't I just use water? Realistically, yes. For most of the recipes in this book you can use chicken stock, beef stock, veal stock, vegetable stock, pork stock, or water. (I wouldn't use fish stock.) If you're using store-bought stock, more power to you. Just make sure you're using low-sodium if you can find it.*

5. Using tongs, remove the beef bones and place them in the same pan you used to roast them. Use a table knife or chopsticks to extract as much marrow as possible, returning it to the broth. Remove the vegetables with the tongs. Strain the stock, if desired, and allow to cool.

Sipping Broth

Makes 1 cup (250ml)

1 cup (250ml) Beef Stock (page 38)

¼ teaspoon Himalayan pink salt

Juice of 1 lemon

30 turns of freshly ground black pepper

1. In a small saucepan, heat the stock over medium-high heat. Once hot, add the salt, lemon juice, and black pepper. Enjoy warm.

RAGU GENOVESE

1 whole beef shank
(10½ pounds/4.76kg), tied,
with the bone removed and
reserved first (the bone weighs
3½ pounds/1.6kg)

1½ tablespoons (15g) kosher salt

Freshly ground black pepper

8 tablespoons (4 ounces/115g)
unsalted butter

¼ cup (55g) extra-virgin olive oil

1½ pounds (680g) thick-cut
pancetta, finely diced

4½ pounds (2kg) large yellow
onions (8 or 9 onions), finely
diced

8 large carrots, finely diced

11 to 12 celery stalks, finely
diced

14 ounces (400g) cherry
tomatoes, whole

1 (4-ounce/115g) tube double
concentrated tomato paste, or
the equivalent in half-used tubes
cluttering up your fridge

1 bottle (750ml) dry white wine

4 fresh bay leaves

1 quart (1 L) beef stock,
store-bought or homemade
(page 38), or really could be
water in a pinch

1 bunch fresh parsley, leaves
picked and finely chopped

Despite its name, ragu Genovese doesn't hail from Genoa, the Northern Italian port city, but from Naples, the Campanian mecca of all things delicious, in the South. Centered around a beef shank, generously studded with pancetta, and fortified with white wine and mounds of onions that melt to create a sweet, savory, sticky sauce, the ragu is called a Genovese because, in the minds of Neapolitans, it's how their wealthy compatriots in the North ate. I learned to make this version while working at Pizzeria Da Attilio in Naples, from the mother of the pizzaiolo. Traditionally, you use fewer tomatoes than I do here, but I find that without them, the sweetness of the onions is overpowering.

This is a perfect gateway ragu for younger kids, thanks to the sweetness of the onions.

The key to a good Genovese is, maybe obviously, the beef shank, a massive piece of meat that feels almost Flintstonian. Derived from the leg — shank — of a cow, shanks are powerful muscles and need to be braised for a long time to break down. (Shanks are also perfect for beef bourguignon.) I like to use a full shank — you'll have to ask your butcher ahead of time — but two half shanks will work, or even one half shank if you halve the recipe. You can use the Genovese in all sorts of ways. It's good on any type of pasta, particularly a ziti, penne, or a rigatoni. You can sub it for the ragu in baked ziti or lasagna, if you'd like. It's delicious over Simple Fluffy Mashed Potatoes (page 205) and Creamy Polenta (page 220), too.

RECIPE CONTINUES

EQUIPMENT:

FoodSaver (optional) or ziplock
bags with the air removed

Have a helper? Pull
out the snorkeling mask
while chopping onions
for dramatic effect
(and fewer tears).

1. Generously season the beef shank with salt and pepper and set aside on a sheet pan.

2. In a large wide Dutch oven or rondeau, heat the butter and olive oil over high heat until melted, about 2 minutes. (If the butter and oil begin to get too dark, reduce the heat to medium.)

3. Add the beef shank to the pan, browning on all sides, about 1½ minutes per side. (You can use your tongs or the side of the pan to prop up the shank if needed.) Once browned, remove the shank and set it aside.

4. In the same pan, cook the diced pancetta over medium heat, rendering the fat and stirring occasionally. The pancetta should be pink and not yet crispy, about 5 minutes. Add the onions, carrots, and celery to the pan, stirring to coat the vegetables in the pancetta fat. Continue to cook on medium heat until translucent and fragrant, about 20 minutes, stirring occasionally.

5. Add the cherry tomatoes, stirring to combine. Stir in the tomato paste and let cook for 8 or so minutes. Pour in the white wine, stirring to combine. Increase the heat to cook off the alcohol, for a few minutes.

STORAGE: Allow the ragu to cool, then vacuum-seal in 3¼ cup (1½-pound/680g) portions and freeze.

6. Return the beef shank (and collected juices), along with the bone, to the pot and bury it under the vegetable mix. Stir in the bay leaves and beef stock, cover with foil, then with the lid (or a heavy pan or pot). Increase the heat to high and bring to a hard simmer, covered—it's okay to peek—then reduce to medium and allow to steady simmer, uncovered, for 2½ hours.

7. Remove the beef shank to a large bowl and let it rest. Uncover the pot and increase the heat to high, allowing the liquid to reduce for 15 to 20 minutes.

8. Meanwhile, once slightly cool, place the beef shank on a sheet pan, removing the string and chopping the beef shank into bite-sized pieces.

9. Once the liquid has reduced, return the meat to the pot. Reduce the heat to low and allow to simmer uncovered for an additional 1 hour. Remove from the heat and stir in the parsley.

10. Use immediately for Ziti with Ragu Genovese (page 91) or any other pasta.

Beef Shank

When you get a whole beef shank from a butcher, it will come with a large bone—the tibia, to be exact. You can either ask the butcher to remove it and give it to you or have them keep the bone in, but cut the shank in half (so it better fits into the pot). The most important thing is to get the bone home and use it. As the shank slowly braises, all that delicious marrow flows from the bone to the sauce, rendering it rich, glossy, and flavorful.

RAGU BOLOGNESE

8 tablespoons (4 ounces/115g) unsalted butter

1 pound (450g) pancetta, coarsely ground or finely chopped

2 medium yellow onions, cut into large chunks

3 medium carrots, peeled and cut into large chunks

4 celery stalks, cut into large chunks

3 garlic cloves, peeled but whole

2 pounds (910g) lean ground beef

2 pounds (910g) ground pork

2 cups (470ml) red wine

1 (28-ounce/794g) can crushed tomatoes

5 fresh bay leaves, or 3 dried bay leaves

3 tablespoons (48g) coarse sea salt, or 4 tablespoons (40g) kosher salt

EQUIPMENT:

Rondeau, FoodSaver (optional) or ziplock bags with the air removed

When you close your eyes and imagine Sunday dinner, this classic red sauce is likely what you're thinking of. Ragu Bolognese, a combination of beef, pork, and tomato, is a straightforward crowd-pleasing protein-packed meat sauce. In Bologna, where I learned how to make it, ragu is used to accent the noodles. It does not, as is sometimes the case in Italian American cuisine, submerge them. In this recipe, the fat is the conduit for flavor, and the reason this particular sauce is so flavorful is because I use an insane amount of coarsely ground pancetta. If I had my druthers, I'd use strutto (rendered lard) or ground lard. As the sauce simmers, the fat-to-water ratio gets bigger, and by the time you toss this with your pasta, the fat will coat the noodles in delicious flavor.

1. In a rondeau, melt the butter over high heat. Once the butter is melted, add the pancetta to render the fat, until it turns translucent. (You aren't looking for, and do not want, color.)

2. Meanwhile, in a food processor, pulse the onions, carrots, celery, and garlic several times until you have uniform small bits. Work in batches if needed.

3. Once the pancetta fat has been rendered, add the vegetables to the pan. Cook until the vegetables become translucent and the liquid evaporates, 5 to 8 minutes.

There's a lot of stirring the pot in this recipe, a perfect task for a little sous-chef. A longer than usual wooden spoon helps protect smaller arms from burns.

4. Add the beef and pork, breaking them up with the back of a wooden spoon. Add the red wine and cook for 10 to 15 minutes to cook off the alcohol.

5. Add the tomatoes with their liquid, stirring well, then fill the tomato can with water and add that as well along with the bay leaves. Add the salt and stir. Reduce the heat to medium and allow the sauce to simmer lightly for 2 to 3 hours, depending on the size of the pot. Stir every 20 to 30 minutes to make sure nothing sticks to the bottom. Once it seems there's no more liquid in the ragu, it's finished.

6. Remove from the heat, allow to cool slightly, stirring occasionally to emulsify the fat into the ragu. Use immediately for the Tag Ragu (page 95) or any other pasta.

STORAGE: Allow the ragu to cool, then vacuum-seal in 3¼ cup (1½-pound/680g) portions and freeze.

THREE-IN-ONE TOMATO SAUCES

3⅓ cups (790ml) extra-virgin
olive oil

24 garlic cloves (120g) (about
2 or 3 heads), thinly sliced

8 (28-ounce/794g) cans crushed
tomatoes

4 bunches basil
(6½ ounces/180g), leaves picked

¼ cup (40g) kosher salt

Pomodoro, or pomo, is your workhorse sauce. If you make a large pot of it—which you should—keep it in the fridge and it'll come in handy. Besides for Spaghetti Pomo (page 79) or baked ziti or a zillion other pasta dishes, you can add it to stewed meat or use it as a dip for Garlic Bread (page 237). With a sauce so simple, there's no hiding. You have to use really good EVOO (which you should be doing anyway; I use Partanna in our restaurants) and really good tomatoes. I prefer Bianco di Napoli tomatoes, which are quasi-local to me in Northern California and, more important, have the right balance between sugar, acidity, and water.

Picking basil leaves, which releases their fragrance, gets kids involved and open to the idea of "green things." (Since they had to work for them.)

Starting with the basic pomo, you can add chile flakes to make the spicier arrabbiata variation (my ongoing project as a parent is to introduce my kid to spice). By adding the chile flakes and bomba to the sauce early, the heat suffuses it, so it flows and hums on your lips rather than burns.

Arrabbiata is a great way to introduce the *idea* of spiciness to your kid. Start off gentle, just a few flakes, then build.

The third part of this three-in-one sauce is something a little rounder, softer, and more luxurious. Cream gets added to the pomo to make a sort of vodka-less vodka sauce that I'm calling Creamy Tomato.

USE POMODORO FOR:

A 100% Chance of Meatballs (page 146)

Handmade Spinach and Cheese Ravioli (page 118)

Cavatelli with Pork Sausage (page 110)

Spaghetti Pomo (page 79)

Zucchini Parmigiana (page 214)

POMODORO SAUCE:

1. In a large saucepot, heat 2 cups (470ml) of the olive oil over high heat until warm, not hot. Add the garlic and once it starts to sizzle and becomes fragrant, add the tomatoes, the basil, and the salt.

2. Offset the lid and bring to a boil. Once it starts to boil, reduce the heat to medium and keep partially covered. Allow to rapidly simmer for 45 to 60 minutes, depending on the size of your pan, stirring occasionally so the sauce does not scorch. As it cooks, the olive oil should float toward the top.

3. Remove from the heat, add the remaining 1⅓ cups (320ml) olive oil, and slowly mix it in. Stir it for a minute to fully incorporate.

ARRABBIATA SAUCE:

Make the pomodoro sauce as directed, adding ¼ cup (20g) chile flakes and ½ cup (160g) Calabrian chili bomba (see page 293) when you add the canned crushed tomatoes.

CREAMY TOMATO SAUCE:

Make the pomodoro sauce as directed, stirring in 2 cups (470ml) heavy cream in the last step. Cook together and reduce until it coats the back of a spoon.

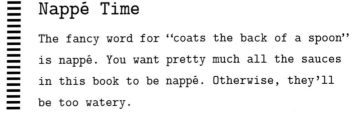

Nappé Time

The fancy word for ''coats the back of a spoon'' is nappé. You want pretty much all the sauces in this book to be nappé. Otherwise, they'll be too watery.

SOUPS

STEWS

SOUPS ARE EASY-TO-MAKE CROWD-PLEASERS. THE effort-to-payoff ratio is ridiculous. Start with a base—most of my soups begin as garlic and onion in a pot softened with butter and olive oil—and build on it, using stock (page 36 or page 38), or water if you just can't be bothered, as the medium for the flavor.

These aren't necessarily quick or small recipes. If I'm going to the trouble of making a soup, I want it to last, with enough for me to give to my mom. Make a big enough pot and it will save your ass all week. (In a sense, soups and stews are batch-cooking, too.) You can easily scale these recipes up or down; they all freeze well, so double or triple them, depending on the size of your pot and ambition. Many of them are even better the next day, when all the ingredients have had ample time to commingle their flavors.

A note on stocks: If you don't want to make your own stock, that's okay. No judgment. Two things: One, look for low-sodium or no salt added. Two, don't get anything with sugar in it or ingredients you don't understand. Words like chicken, rosemary, and onion are good. Words like monowhateverthefuck are not.

MELTDOWN
MEAL

BUTTERY TOMATO SOUP

¼ cup (60ml) extra-virgin olive oil

2 tablespoons (30g) unsalted butter

½ medium yellow onion, sliced

1 head garlic, cloves separated and thinly sliced

2 (28-ounce/794g) cans crushed tomatoes

1 bunch basil, leaves picked

1 tablespoon (10g) kosher salt, plus up to ½ tablespoon (5g) to taste

EQUIPMENT:

Blender (Vitamix, regular, or stick)

This simple and extremely quick tomato soup is delicious on its own, but the Hall to its Oates is the grilled cheese sandwich (page 226). Tomato and cheese, what could be better?

This is the soup for a cold and rainy day, when there's water in your socks and you missed your train. It's the soup to make to snuggle up to a Christmas movie (even if it's not Christmas and/or you're not Christian) and concede the day.

This soup keeps in the fridge for a week and also freezes well, so I often double the recipe to make a larger batch.

1. Heat a saucepot over high heat. Once hot, add the olive oil and butter to melt. Once the foaming has subsided, add the onion and garlic and stir until fragrant and beginning to color, about 2 minutes. Stir in the canned tomatoes, basil, and salt and cook for 4 to 5 minutes, stirring occasionally.

2. Carefully transfer the mixture to a blender (see Something I Learned the Hard Way, page 54). It should fit in one batch. If not, blend in two. If you are using a stick blender, you can blend directly in the pot. Slowly blend, starting on low and working your way up to a higher speed. If you want a smoother

Kids can definitely help with the picking of herbs and the pot stirring, but not the blending. See Something I Learned the Hard Way, page 54.

RECIPE CONTINUES

soup, blend longer. Feel free to blend for less time for more texture.

3. Carefully remove the blender pitcher and season the soup with additional salt, if desired. Return the soup to the pot and enjoy right away or cool down and save for later.

Something I Learned the Hard Way

Blending hot liquids can be dangerous. Always make sure the blender is in the OFF position before you plug it in. Plug the blender in and then add liquid to the pitcher. When using a standard blender, make sure to remove the steam valve in the lid before blending in order to relieve pressure. Cover the lid with a clean towel and always start slow. I've seen more than one young cook go to the emergency room with burns on their face from exploding blenders full of hot soup.

STRACCIATELLA

8 cups (1.9L) chicken stock, store-bought or homemade (page 36)

4 ounces (115g) Parmigiano-Reggiano cheese, freshly grated (about 1¼ cups)

¼ cup (60ml) extra-virgin olive oil

4 large eggs

30 turns of freshly ground black pepper

4 cups packed spinach (8 ounces/225g), roughly chopped

2 tablespoons (20g) kosher salt

Crusty bread, for serving

Stracciatella—which just means ''little shreds''—can also refer to a gelato made with chocolate shavings as well as a soft cheese made of cream and shreds of mozzarella, so it is possible to have a Stracciatella Stracciatella Stracciatella meal, for funsies.

Gently stirring in the egg mixture—and watching it turn opaque as it cooks—is the most fun part of making this soup, for you and your kids.

Stracciatella, a Roman soup of broth, eggs, greens, and cheese, takes nearly no time to make, has just a few ingredients (most of which you'll likely have lying around), and requires the most basic technique. (If you can boil and stir, you can perfect this soup.) I like to think of stracciatella as an Italian egg drop soup, protein-rich and fortified with as many greens as you can fit in. (I used spinach, but kale or chard would be great, too, though they're a little tough, so you'll have to cook longer until they're tender.) Because the cheese is mixed into the soup, this is one of the rare soups where I'll only make as much as can be eaten at the time.

1. In a large pot, bring the chicken stock to a boil over high heat.

2. Place the parmesan in a bowl. Pour the olive oil over the grated cheese. Add the eggs. Add the pepper. With a wooden spoon, gently beat the eggs with the other ingredients, making sure not to overmix. Set aside.

3. Once the stock is boiling, reduce the heat to low (do not turn off). Add the spinach and salt, increase the heat to high, and bring back to a boil.

4. Remove from the heat. Pour the cheese mixture into the soup. With the same wooden spoon, gently stir, taking care not to break up the curds. The soup should not be returned to the heat after the egg and cheese have been added. Serve immediately with crusty bread.

TUSCAN SAUSAGE, BEAN, AND KALE SOUP

½ cup (120ml) extra-virgin olive oil

1 pound (450g) Italian sausages, casings removed

4 garlic cloves, minced

3 medium carrots, diced

4 celery stalks, diced

1 large yellow onion, diced

1 bunch lacinato (Tuscan) kale (10 ounces/285g), thick stems removed, leaves roughly chopped

2 (12.7-ounce/360g) jars Italian corona beans, undrained

1 (28-ounce/794g) can whole peeled tomatoes

2 quarts (1.9L) chicken stock, store-bought or homemade (page 36)

1 tightly packed cup (75g) chopped Italian parsley

1 sprig fresh rosemary, leaves picked

½ teaspoon chile flakes

Grated zest and juice of 2 lemons

2 heaping tablespoons (25g) kosher salt

Try to get carrots with their greens attached. The tops make great handles for little hands to hold while peeling.

A traditional zuppa Toscana is already hearty, meant to fortify the peasants who first made it. This is a supercharged version with a ton of sausage in it. I make this around twelve times a year. I love it. My kid loves it. It hits every note you want it to hit. The pork fat renders, imbuing the soup with flavor, while the beans add a creamy texture and the kale adds loads of nutritional content. But this soup is more about the liquid-to-solid ratio than it is about any specific ingredients. So I officially give you agency to fuck with this recipe. Don't have kale? Use escarole or spinach or Swiss chard or whatever you can. Want less lemon? OK! It took me three or four times making this soup to get the balance I like. Bring it to a friend. Take it to a grandparent. It's an instant friendship soup.

Kale is full of a whole alphabet of vitamins (A, B_6, C, K), as well as folate, fiber, and carotenoids.

1. In a soup pot, heat the olive oil over high heat until it shimmers. Add the Italian sausage and cook until almost browned.

2. Stir in the garlic, carrots, celery, and onion and cook until they are fragrant and start to slightly soften, 4 to 5 minutes. Stir in the kale and cook for 2 to 3 minutes. Add the corona beans and their liquid and stir. Add the canned tomatoes,

FOR SERVING:

Extra-virgin olive oil

Parmigiano-Reggiano cheese

Freshly ground black pepper

STORAGE: Allow to cool, then store in an airtight container in the refrigerator for up to 1 week.

crushing them by hand as you add them to the pot. Stir in the chicken stock and cook at a lively simmer for 20 minutes.

3. Stir in the parsley, rosemary, chile flakes, and lemon zest. Add the salt and lemon juice.

4. To serve, finish with olive oil, parmesan, and black pepper.

TUSCAN SAUSAGE,
BEAN, AND KALE SOUP,
page 56

WEEKNIGHT
MEAL

VEGETABLE MINESTRONE

10 tablespoons extra-virgin olive oil

1 head garlic, cloves separated and coarsely chopped

1 medium yellow onion, chopped

9 small carrots, such as Nantes (10 ounces/285g total), medium-diced

4 celery stalks, medium-diced

1 large red bell pepper, medium-diced

13 ounces (370g) green beans, chopped to the size of peas

2 zucchini (1 pound/450g total), medium-diced

1 (28-ounce/794g) can whole peeled tomatoes, undrained

2 (15-ounce/425g) cans kidney beans, undrained

Sliced peel of 2 lemons (see Note)

1½ tablespoons fresh oregano leaves, chopped

8 ounces (225g) elbow macaroni or any other small, bite-sized pasta shape

1 cup (50g) chopped fresh Italian parsley

Kosher salt

¼ cup (60ml) fresh lemon juice

1 big ol' chunk Parmigiano-Reggiano cheese, for serving

Freshly ground black pepper, for serving

A minestrone is a cost-effective and soothing way to . . . subvert your child's will and then clown them afterward for eating all the vegetables they're always saying they don't like. Minestrone is essentially just chopped vegetables in a delicious tomato-based broth. It's also a great way to mise en place with your kid.

Mise en place is a French phrase that basically just means all the prep work you have to do to start cooking. In this case—and actually in many cases—it means lots and lots of chopping vegetables.

1. In a Dutch oven or large soup pot, heat 6 tablespoons of the olive oil over medium heat until it shimmers. Add the garlic and allow to sweat for a minute, being careful not to let it brown. Add the onion, sweat for 2 to 3 minutes. Add the vegetables one at a time, letting each one sweat: carrots (2 minutes), celery (1 minute), bell pepper (1 minute), green beans (1 minute), zucchini (1 minute). Then add the tomatoes and juice, breaking up the tomatoes with the back of a spoon. Refill the can with water and add the water. Add the kidney beans with their liquid, followed by the lemon peel and oregano. Add the pasta to the soup, making sure to scrape the bottom when stirring to ensure it doesn't stick. Add the chopped parsley and season with salt.

There are plenty of opportunities here to chop things with your little sous. Don't worry too much how uniformly they're chopped. (There's no rule saying your kid can't do an initial cut with a kid's knife and then you do a once over when they're done.)

2. Bring to a rapid simmer over medium-high heat and cook until the pasta is done, 8 to 10 minutes. Add the lemon juice and stir. Finish with the remaining 3 tablespoons olive oil.

3. Serve in bowls with grated parmesan and black pepper.

NOTE: *So technically, I'm saying the sliced peel, but I mean the sliced zest. The peel of the lemon is the yellow part (zest) and the white part (albedo). However, and frankly confusingly, I want you to zest using a peeler (see page 290) and not a zester, so, I mean, whatever. You basically want all the essential oils of the lemon that are found in the zest but not the boring and bitter albedo. Get it however you can.*

CHICKEN ENCHILADA STEW

⅓ cup (80ml) extra-virgin olive oil

2 pounds (910g) boneless, skinless chicken thighs, cut into quarters

1½ pounds (680g) Yukon Gold potatoes, scrubbed and halved (cut in quarters if large)

1½ tablespoons chili powder

1 green bell pepper, diced

1 head cauliflower (12 ounces/340g), cut into medium florets

2 (15-ounce/425g) jars green enchilada sauce

1 cup (250ml) chicken stock, store-bought or homemade (page 36)

1 bunch cilantro (3 ounces/90g), leaves and stems, roughly chopped

1 bunch Italian parsley (40g), leaves roughly chopped

1 bunch green onions (3½ ounces/95g), thinly sliced

2 tablespoons fresh lime juice

Kosher salt

FOR SERVING:

Avocado, sliced or diced

Sour cream

Shredded Monterey Jack cheese

Nearly every taqueria I walk into has chile verde on the menu and since I walk into a lot of taquerias, I eat a lot of it. How can you not fall for the rich slightly spicy flavor of the chiles, the long-stewed meat (usually pork), and a parade of condiments: avocado! sour cream! shredded cheese! This recipe is a down and dirty home version, with more shortcuts than a keyboard. A couple of cans of enchilada sauce form the base. (My favorite brand is Siete.) Instead of pork, I subbed in chicken thighs, which are a forgiving meat and nearly impossible to overcook. Most of the prep work can be done as the thighs cook in the pan. As the flavors commingle, everything in the stew, including the cauliflower (an unusual but inoffensive and nutritious addition), is infused with flavor.

When it comes to cutting, not all vegetables are easy for kids or adults. Potatoes, though—and really anything solid and of regular shape—are a wonderful introduction to knife skills.

1. In a rondeau, heat the olive oil over high heat. Add the chicken pieces, cooking in one even layer. Allow the pieces to get some caramelization, about 5 minutes. If the chicken sticks to the pot, don't stress out—just stir to unstick. Stir in the potatoes and cook for about 2 minutes.

2. Stir in the chili powder and fry in the oil for 1 to 2 minutes. Stir in the bell pepper and cauliflower and cook

EQUIPMENT:

Rondeau

STORAGE: Allow to cool, then store in an airtight container in the refrigerator for up to 1 week.

for 1 minute. Add the enchilada sauce, stir to coat all ingredients, and cook for 2 to 3 minutes. Add the chicken stock, cover, and cook over high heat, uncovering to stir occasionally, for 20 minutes.

3. Uncover, and stir in the cilantro, parsley, and green onions. Stir in the lime juice. Remove from the heat and add salt to taste.

4. Serve with avocado, sour cream, and shredded cheese.

Cauliflower, like other cruciferous vegetables, is rich in choline, a nutrient that supports brain development, especially in children.

TURKEY CHILI

FOR THE CHILI SPICE MIX:

1½ tablespoons chili powder

1 tablespoon smoked paprika

1½ teaspoons ground cumin

1 teaspoon onion powder

½ teaspoon garlic powder

3 tablespoons (30g) kosher salt

1 teaspoon freshly ground black pepper

FOR THE CHILI:

⅓ cup (80ml) extra-virgin olive oil

3 pounds (1.4kg) ground turkey

2 tablespoons tomato paste

4 celery stalks, sliced lengthwise and finely diced

2 medium red onions, medium-diced

1 head garlic, chopped

1 large red bell pepper, cut into large squares

1 large green bell pepper, cut into large squares

1 jalapeño pepper (20g), seeded and medium-diced

2 large Roma tomatoes, medium-diced

2 (15-ounce/425g) cans kidney beans, undrained

Growing up in a Soviet émigré household, classic American dishes like chili or meatloaf were not on the menu. It wasn't until culinary school, and when I began eating at the Greek diners in upstate New York near the Culinary Institute, that I was first exposed to chili or shepherd's pie or apple pie. And it wasn't really until staff meals at restaurants that I fell in love with them. This version of turkey chili is heavy on the vegetables and on the protein. My biggest challenge with Helena and Niko is how to deliver them enough protein. (I also need a high-protein diet.) I'm conscious not to always defer to pork and beef. What I love about this chili is that it's full of protein but, because turkey is so lean, it isn't heavy or greasy. To be honest, though, the recipe works just as well with beef or pork. Or, if you want, a combination of all three. The result is a versatile and long-lasting dinner that goes well with rice, on its own, with roasted potatoes, with some veggies, or, if you're feeling decadent, over French fries with melted cheese.

Yeah, 22 ingredients is a lot, but consolidate away. If you want to just use green bell peppers, fine. If you want to use a premade chili spice mix (instead of all the spices), have at it. The idea of this chili is that it's delicious, not that it's hard.

Turkey is high in protein and full of vitamins B_3 (cells!), B_6 (metabolism!), and B_{12} (DNA!).

RECIPE AND INGREDIENTS CONTINUE

3 cups (700ml) chicken or beef stock, store-bought or homemade (page 36 and page 38), or water

Juice of 2 limes (¼ cup/60ml)

1 bunch green onions, sliced

1 bunch cilantro, leaves and stems, finely chopped

FOR SERVING:

Sour cream

Shredded cheddar cheese

Sliced green onion

STORAGE: Allow to cool, then store in an airtight container in the refrigerator for up to 1 week.

1. **Make the chili spice mix:** In a small bowl, mix the chili pepper, smoked paprika, cumin, onion powder, garlic powder, salt, and pepper until well combined.

2. **Make the chili:** In a large stockpot, heat the olive oil over high heat until it shimmers, about 1 minute. Add the turkey and cook for 5 minutes, breaking it up with a wooden spoon into smaller chunks. Add the spice mix to the meat and stir. Add the tomato paste and stir, then add the celery, onions, garlic, bell peppers, jalapeño, and tomatoes and cook for 4 minutes. Add the beans and their liquid, stirring until combined.

3. Stir in the stock, bring to a simmer, and allow to cook for 1 hour, stirring occasionally to ensure that the chili isn't sticking to the bottom of the pot.

4. Add the lime juice, sliced green onions, and cilantro. Cook for 10 more minutes, stirring occasionally. Remove from the heat. Taste and adjust salt as desired.

5. Let the chili sit for 10 minutes, then serve with accoutrements.

JEWISH MOTHER'S CHICKEN SOUP

PROJECT COOKING

1 whole chicken (3 to 3½ pounds/ 1.4 to 1.6kg)

2 tablespoons (30g) unsalted butter

1¼ pounds (575g) yellow onions (about 2 large), diced

3 large carrots, diced

4 celery stalks, diced

5 garlic cloves, sliced

Thinly sliced peel of 1 lemon

8 cups (1.9L) chicken stock, store-bought or homemade (page 36)

2 bunches green onions (5 ounces/140g), thinly sliced

2 bunches fresh dill (3½ ounces/ 100g), finely chopped

Juice of 4 lemons (1 cup/240ml)

Kosher salt

60 turns of freshly ground black pepper

Everybody has a Jewish mother, or their version of one—someone who loves you in their own intense, human, complicated but affirming way. My own Jewish mother, Mama Galina, is a woman who exudes love and emotion at every turn. When I felt sick as a kid— and even now—she would drop everything to come care for me. She'd pump me full of cloves of garlic, honey, home-remedy concoctions. I'd be sent to bed to rest, but the bedroom door would open every fifteen minutes for a different type of tea to choke down. She loved me aggressively (maybe why I'm attracted to jiujitsu). This soup is a culmination and embodiment of that maternal care that I make for Helena when she's got a cold. To me, it literally is the taste of being loved. I've added a few of my own touches—more dill, more lemon, homemade stock if I have it—but its underlying function is still the same: to put all your love, your care, your comfort in a bowl and serve it to anyone who needs it.

There are plenty of opportunities here, from peeling to dicing to stirring, to work side by side. The best part is that it always ends with a steaming bowl of soup.

Chicken soup is such an effective vehicle for health because all the vitamins and nutrients from the meat and vegetables are retained in the broth and consumed, as opposed to when they're sautéed and left behind in the pan.

1. Wash the chicken in scalding hot water under a faucet for 2 minutes. Remove any stray feathers and schmutz, place

RECIPE CONTINUES

the chicken in a large stockpot, and add enough cold water to submerge it by 2 inches.

2. Bring the liquid to a boil over high heat. Reduce the heat to a lively simmer and let simmer for 45 minutes, skimming any foam on the surface with a slotted spoon. Remove the whole chicken with tongs. Set aside on a cutting board. Discard the water but hold onto the stockpot. Once cooled, pick the meat from the bones and set aside in a bowl. Discard the skin and bones.

3. In the large stockpot, melt the butter over high heat. When the foaming subsides, add the onions, carrots, celery, garlic, and lemon peel to the pot. Stirring occasionally, allow the vegetables to sweat, about 20 minutes.

4. Once the vegetables are translucent and fragrant, stir in the chicken stock, bring to a high simmer, and simmer for 20 minutes.

5. Stir in the picked chicken meat, the green onions, and dill and cook for 10 minutes.

6. Stir in the lemon juice. After a minute or so, add salt to taste. After another minute, stir in the black pepper. Cook for 10 minutes. Reduce the heat to low and allow to simmer for 10 minutes. Serve immediately.

PROJECT
COOKING

IMMUNITY SOUP

1 whole chicken (3½ to
4 pounds/1.6 to 1.8kg)

1½ cups (360ml) extra-virgin
olive oil

1 large knob (3½ ounces/100g)
fresh ginger, peeled and minced

1 head garlic (3½ ounces/100g)

1 leek (1 pound/455g), sliced into
thin rings

1 cup (200g) uncooked brown rice

2 bunches fresh Italian parsley
(100g), leaves picked and
chopped (2 cups packed)

2 sprigs fresh oregano, leaves
picked

5 quarts (5L) chicken stock,
store-bought or homemade
(page 36)

2 large bunches kale
(10½ ounces/300g), stems and
midribs removed, chopped

2 bunches spinach (6 ounces/
170g each), chopped

Thinly sliced peel of 3 lemons

2 (15-ounce/425g) cans
chickpeas, undrained

3 zucchini (1 pound
7 ounces/650g total), diced

¼ cup (40g) kosher salt

60 turns of freshly ground black
pepper

Juice of 6 lemons (¾ cup/180ml)

When someone in my house is feeling so sick that even the restorative properties of Jewish Mother's Chicken Soup (page 67) can't heal them, it's time to call in the big guns: Immunity Soup. (I mean, yes, also cold and flu medicine.) Immunity soup is the holy grail of bacteria-killing virus-suppressing fascism-quelling and it also happens to be incredibly nourishing. It's super comforting and packs so much nutritional value that you can taste the vitality.

If you're making this soup, your kids are likely sick. My tip is to make a big batch because chances are you're probably next. Sorry.

1. Wash the chicken in scalding hot water under a faucet for 2 minutes. Remove any stray feathers and schmutz, place the chicken in a large stockpot, and add enough cold water to submerge it by 2 inches.

2. Bring the liquid to a boil over high heat. Reduce the heat to a lively simmer and let simmer for 45 minutes, skimming any foam on the surface with a slotted spoon. Remove the whole chicken with tongs. Set aside on a cutting board. Discard the water but hold onto the stockpot. Once cooled, pick the meat from the bones and set aside in a bowl. Discard the skin and bones.

3. In the large stockpot, heat 1 cup (240ml) of the olive oil over high heat until it shimmers. Add the ginger, garlic, and leek and sauté until aromatic, about 7 minutes.

EQUIPMENT:

Stick blender or blender

STORAGE: Allow to cool, then store in an airtight container in the refrigerator for up to 1 week.

4. Stir in the rice and toast for 3 to 4 minutes. Stir in the parsley and oregano. Add the picked chicken meat to the stockpot. Then add enough chicken stock to cover the chicken entirely. Bring to a hard boil over high heat and cook for 25 minutes.

5. Add the kale, spinach, lemon peel, chickpeas and their liquid, and zucchini to the soup. Season with the salt and pepper, then stir in the lemon juice.

6. Remove 4 cups of the soup from the pot and carefully place in a blender. Remove the steam valve in the lid, cover the lid with a clean towel, and start slow. Blend on high until smooth. Pour back into the soup.

7. Remove from the heat, finish with the remaining ½ cup (120ml) olive oil, and serve immediately.

PASTA

PASTA IS PARADISE FOR A PARENT. WHAT BETTER weaves together protein and vegetables than starchy noodles, a delivery system that creates harmony between parents and their children? With the right pasta preparation, you know your kid is getting a significant amount of sustenance; they know they're getting noodles. It's a win-win situation.

Though I made pasta in culinary school, my pasta enlightenment came from a man named Enrique, the pasta maker at Shea Gallante's Cru in New York City. Enrique handcrafted the pasta shapes with as much skill and attention as is traditionally devoted to more "prestigious" recipes. Later on, while rolling pasta side by side with Los Angeles pasta wizard Evan Funke, I came to understand Enrique's devotion even more deeply. Pasta gives you as much love as you give it. I have yet to find its upper limit.

My most recent pasta awakening came when I started cooking pasta as a dad. I had made pasta in its highest form. Now I was learning exactly how versatile pasta could be. On one hand, making fresh dough can be an entire family activity. On the other, using dried or extruded pasta and some batch-made sauce, you can have a home-cooked meal on the table in less than 20 minutes. Pasta can be simplified for the pickiest eaters or sophisticated for the more daring palate. It brooks experimentation. It rewards technique. It pleases all.

Notes on Cooking Pasta

Your water should be boiling and be salty like the sea. Don't be impatient with the temperature or stingy with the salinity. I know it's hard.

Leave extra time to cook the noodles in the pan with whatever sauce or *condimenti* are accompanying them. Follow the lower number suggested on the box for a cooking time, and then reduce that by 1 minute.

When the pasta is simmering with the sauce, it is like a child at its most malleable and most able to accept input. That's when you take it off the stove and stir it with the sauce so the fat stains the surface and the flavor penetrates the cell structure.

Finish the pasta with style, flourish, and wisdom. Add grated cheese off the heat and don't turn it back on. (The heat will denature the proteins.) EVOO at this point will really brighten a pasta up, adding a tremendous impact that can't happen if you put it in at the beginning. If freshly ground black pepper is appropriate, this is the moment when it sings.

Notes on Storing and Reheating Pasta

As with all leftovers, the best thing you can do is let the pasta cool to room temperature. Place the pasta in a Tupperware, refrigerate it with the lid offset so cool air can flow in and heat out. In the morning, pop the lid back on. That will give you the longest shelf life. If, in the morning, you see condensation on the lid, you know you refrigerated it too soon. Be more patient next time.

TO REHEAT: For those of you who microwave, microwave the pasta covered, so the steam remains inside the container and the pasta doesn't dry out. If you, like me, don't have a microwave, a really easy way to reheat pasta is to turn an oven on at 350°F (180°C). Line a sheet pan with aluminum foil. Place the pasta directly on the foil, fold up the sides to make a steaming envelope, and cook for 20 minutes. Finish with olive oil and cheese, if desired.

SPAGHETTI POMO

MELTDOWN
MEAL

6 cups (1.4L) Pomodoro Sauce
(page 47)

3 tablespoons extra-virgin olive
oil, plus more for drizzling

2 garlic cloves, thinly sliced

½ cup (70g) kosher salt, for the
pasta water

1 pound (455g) dried spaghetti

Grated Parmigiano-Reggiano
cheese, for serving

Basil leaves, for serving

Talk about the workhorse of workhorses; spaghetti pomodoro can please the most sophisticated food critic, be they eight years old or forty-three. The key is pulling the spaghetti out of the boiling water and putting it into the sauce alongside an extraordinarily flavorful olive oil. The acidity, lycopene, sugars, and umami from the tomatoes, and olive oil meld with the pungency of the garlic and the basil. There are many arguments for whether to use grated parmesan or pecorino or a blend of the two. I've used both, but I tend to lean to parmesan because I prefer the fattiness and nuttiness. Spaghetti pomo is so simple, democratic, and inexpensive. I could make this dish for a president or for my daughter or for someone who has never eaten outside chain restaurants in their life and they all will be equally blown away.

This is a quick dish with hardly any time for helpers and without much to do. But letting your kids—or your friends— finish the pasta with their chosen amount of cheese gives them a sense of autonomy. No matter how illusory.

1. If the pomodoro sauce is frozen, thaw it. You can heat it over medium heat in a pot or run it under hot water.

2. In a large sauté pan, heat the olive oil over medium-high heat. Add the garlic and sauté until fragrant, about 1 minute.

RECIPE CONTINUES

Add the pomodoro sauce, bring to a light simmer, and then turn down the heat.

3. Bring a large pot of water to a boil and add the kosher salt until it's salty like the sea. Add the spaghetti and cook 1 to 2 minutes shy of al dente according to the package directions. Right before the pasta is done cooking, reserve ½ cup (120ml) of pasta water.

4. Use tongs to lift the pasta out of the pot and into the pan with the sauce. Add the reserved pasta water. Increase the heat to medium-high and stir with the tongs to emulsify the sauce with the pasta. Continue to do so for about 3 minutes, or until the sauce looks like it is sticking to the noodles.

5. Serve with grated parmesan, basil leaves, and a drizzle of olive oil.

PASTA E FAGIOLI

MELTDOWN
MEAL

Kosher salt

½ cup (120ml) extra-virgin olive oil, plus more to finish

1 pound (500g) thick-cut pancetta, cut into 1-inch cubes (2 tightly packed cups)

¼ cup (20g) garlic cloves, thinly sliced

5 medium onions, diced

5 medium carrots, diced

6 celery stalks, diced

Thinly sliced peel and juice of 2 lemons (¼ cup/60ml)

2 sprigs fresh rosemary, picked and chopped

4 sprigs fresh thyme, picked

2 (14-ounce/400g) cans butter beans, undraincd

1 pound (455g) conchiglie or similar shaped pasta shells

1 bunch Italian parsley (2 ounces/65g), picked and chopped

2 cups (8 ounces/220g) freshly grated Parmigiano-Reggiano cheese, plus more for serving

Pasta (*pasta*) with beans (*fagioli*) is found throughout Italy, with immense variation region to region, town to town. The same reasons it's popular there are why it's popular at my house. The ingredients are affordable and protein-rich, the process astonishingly easy, and the end result delicious. I always think of pasta e fagioli as the quintessential winter recipe, but it's perfect for anytime you need a little comfort. The creaminess of the beans instantly soothes. This recipe calls for more lemon juice than seems sane, but trust me. The acidity of the lemon gives each bite a brightness and lightness, cutting through the richness of the beans, the pancetta, and the parmesan.

Set up an assembly line for herb picking. This is an opportunity to involve multiple kids in the cooking process.

1. Bring a large pot of water to a boil, adding about ½ cup (70g) kosher salt to the water until it's salty like the sea.

2. In a large heavy-bottomed pot, heat the olive oil over medium heat for about 1 minute. Add the pancetta and cook until it starts to brown and become crispy, about 4 to 5 minutes. Add the garlic and stir consistently until it becomes fragrant. Add the onions and sweat them for 1 minute. Add the carrots and celery and cook for about 4 minutes. Add the lemon peel, rosemary, thyme, and beans and their liquid and cook for 30 seconds. Turn off the heat.

RECIPE CONTINUES

3. Add the pasta to the boiling water and stir to avoid sticking. Cover the pot until the water returns to a rapid boil. Cook the pasta for 1 or 2 minutes shy of al dente according to the package directions. Use a slotted spoon to scoop the pasta out of the water and add it to the beans and vegetables. Reserve 2 cups (500ml) of the pasta water.

4. Increase the heat to high under the pasta and beans. Add the reserved pasta water, the lemon juice, parsley, and 1 tablespoon (9g) kosher salt. Cook the pasta over high heat for 2 minutes. Add a splash of olive oil to finish.

5. Remove from the heat and add the parmesan. Stir the pasta constantly for 1 minute. This will thicken the pasta and create the sauce. Serve immediately and finish the top of each plate with more parmesan.

SPICY RIGATONI WITH TOMATO, CREAM, AND ROASTED PEPPERS

¼ cup (60ml) extra-virgin olive oil

5 to 7 garlic cloves, thinly sliced

1 (16-ounce/454g) jar roasted red peppers, roughly sliced into 1½-inch (4cm) strips

1 large tomato (see Note), cut into large chunks and white core removed

½ cup basil leaves

1 (15-ounce/425g) can crushed tomatoes

2 tablespoons Calabrian chili bomba (see page 293)

1 cup (250ml) heavy cream

Kosher salt

1 pound (455g) rigatoni

Freshly ground black pepper

½ bunch Italian parsley (1 ounce/30g), finely chopped

Freshly grated Parmigiano-Reggiano cheese, for serving

EQUIPMENT:

Rondeau

Spicy is a relative term, especially with kids, who can be extra sensitive to spice. It makes sense. A child's pain receptors—which like adults' are activated by capsaicin, the active compound in chiles—are more sensitive. But this dish is a great way to introduce spice not as a binary—you like it or you don't—but as a spectrum. The sweetness of the cream serves to cut through the spice of the bomba. But the bomba, one of my favorite ingredients, also tempers the hotness with a complex mix of ingredients like garlic confit and fermented chili that rounds out the spice. It's less a punch and more a vibration. (You can also use crushed Calabrian chilis in oil if you can't find bomba.) You know your family best, so feel free to experiment with the amount of spice you add.

Once you get comfortable, you can cook the sauce while the rigatoni is cooking. But when you're just starting, do the pasta first and *then* the sauce.

Fermented chilis, as in the bomba, are not only delicious (for me), but capsaicin also has anti-inflammatory, analgesic, and antioxidant properties (for everyone).

1. Heat a rondeau over high heat. Once hot, add the olive oil. When the olive oil is shimmering, add the garlic and allow it to slightly brown, about 1 minute. Add the roasted red peppers, fresh tomato, basil, and canned crushed

RECIPE CONTINUES

tomatoes, stirring after each addition. Add the chili bomba, if desired. Stir in the cream, then add 1 tablespoon (10g) kosher salt, stirring to combine. Remove from the heat and set aside.

2. Bring a large pot of water to a boil and add ½ cup (70g) kosher salt until it's salty like the sea. Add the rigatoni and cook until al dente according to the package directions. Using a spider strainer, a sieve, or a colander, transfer the rigatoni directly into the sauce (it's okay if some water gets into the sauce).

3. Return the rigatoni and sauce to the heat, stirring constantly to make sure nothing sticks to the bottom of the pan. Bring to a simmer and then remove from the heat, while continuing to stir. Add a few turns of freshly ground black pepper. Stir constantly for another 1 minute to emulsify the sauce. Add the chopped parsley and stir in. Serve with parmesan.

SPAGHETTI AGLIO, OLIO, E PEPPERONCINO

½ cup (70g) kosher salt

1 pound (455g) spaghetti

½ cup (120ml) extra-virgin olive oil, plus more for serving

1 head garlic, cloves separated and thinly sliced

2 tablespoons Calabrian chili bomba (see page 293)

30g/30ml juice of 1 large lemon and slivered peel

2 bunches fresh parsley (75g), leaves picked and chopped (1¼ packed cups)

½ cup (45g) freshly grated Parmigiano-Reggiano cheese

EQUIPMENT:

Rondeau

It's hard to think of a simpler, cheaper, or more delicious dinner than a bowl of spaghetti AOP. This Neapolitan dish is the prototypical example of *cucina povera,* or "poor man's cuisine." And what kept Campanian families well fed keeps mine, too. You'll probably find all of these ingredients in even the least well-stocked pantry: dried pasta, olive oil, garlic, and chile flakes are all long lasting. Even parsley, when kept in a mason jar with water, can last up to 3 weeks. I've added a few twists—so apologies to all the purists and literalists out there—including lemon (a Nayfeld necessity), Calabrian chili bomba (which adds a deeper flavor than the traditional chile flakes), and cheese, which gives the dish a luxuriously creamy finish, and gives kids at least the semblance of autonomy.

Mixing the ingredients into the pasta at the end of the recipe is an opportunity for fun and teamwork. One kid throws; one kid stirs.

1. Bring a large pot of water to a boil and add the kosher salt until it's salty like the sea. Add the spaghetti, stir with tongs to make sure the pasta doesn't stick to the bottom, and cook to 1 minute shy of al dente according to the package directions.

RECIPE CONTINUES

NOTE: *Herbs kept in a mason jar with water in it can last up to 3 weeks in the fridge.*

2. When the pasta is about 5 minutes from being done, heat a rondeau over high heat. Add the olive oil. Once the oil is shimmering, add the garlic and stir. The garlic should sizzle when it hits the pan but should not take on any color. Cook for 1 to 1½ minutes.

3. Add the chili bomba to the pan and stir. It will sizzle and turn the oil orange. Cook for 30 seconds. Stir in the lemon peel and parsley and cook for about 1 minute.

4. Using tongs, pull the spaghetti out of the cooking water and transfer directly to the rondeau. Reserve ½ cup (120ml) pasta water. Stir the pasta with a wooden spoon and cook for 2½ minutes.

5. Remove from the heat. Add the reserved pasta water, lemon juice, and parmesan and stir with the wooden spoon, vigorously rocking the pan back and forth while stirring to emulsify the sauce for about a minute.

6. Serve with a drizzle of olive oil on top.

ZITI WITH RAGU GENOVESE

MELTDOWN
MEAL

½ cup (70g) kosher salt, plus more if needed

1½ pounds (700g) Ragu Genovese (page 41)

1 pound (455g) ziti

4 tablespoons (55g) unsalted butter

2 tablespoons extra-virgin olive oil, plus more for drizzling

Freshly ground black pepper

3 heaping tablespoons freshly grated Parmigiano-Reggiano cheese, plus more for serving

EQUIPMENT:

Rondeau

This is a recipe for when you just want to get dinner on the table. But if you want some kid buy-in, let them grate cheese and finish each plate with olive oil.

Ziti is the traditional pasta shape for ragu Genovese, most often used in Naples and in Campania. I am a big proponent of sticking with the traditional shapes just so I can see for myself what the hubbub is all about. But if I don't have ziti, I might use a longer rigatoni. Even penne or fusilli would do the trick here. With a ragu like a Genovese or a Bolognese, you want the pasta to be the conduit for the condiment, not to swim in it.

1. If the ragu sauce is frozen, thaw it over medium heat in a rondeau. If it is not frozen, simply warm it in the rondeau over medium heat.

2. Bring a large pot of water to a boil and add the kosher salt until it's salty like the sea. Add the ziti and give it a quick stir so it doesn't stick. Place the lid back on top, offset, and let come to a boil once more. Now's a good time to keep an eye on the water since it can boil over quickly. Once it comes to a rapid boil, remove the lid. Cook the pasta for 2 minutes shy of al dente according to the package directions.

3. Once the pasta is almost done, scoop about ½ cup (120ml) hot pasta water into the ragu. With a spider strainer, scoop the pasta from the boiling water and place directly into the ragu. Increase the heat to high and stir together the pasta and ragu. After 2 minutes, remove from the heat and stir in the butter, olive oil, and a few turns of black pepper. Add kosher salt if needed (the pasta water should have given plenty) and stir in the parmesan, constantly stirring for 30 seconds.

4. Finish with a drizzle of olive oil and another dusting of parmesan.

SPAGHETTI AL LIMONE

½ cup kosher salt (70g), plus more if needed

1 pound (455g) spaghetti

4 tablespoons (55g) unsalted butter

¼ cup/60ml thinly sliced peel and juice of 2 large lemons

1 cup (110g) freshly grated Parmigiano-Reggiano cheese, plus more for serving

Spaghetti al limone is a savior dish. You can make it in 15 minutes, with things you probably have in the fridge anyway and there's no struggle. So when homework needs to get done? Spaghetti al limone. When everyone's already at their limit? Spaghetti al limone. When it's winter and lemons are large and juicy, al limone, and when it's summer and they're still easy to find, al limone. Flavorwise, it's a step up, but a delicious incremental one, from noodles and butter. That's thanks to the titular lemon, *all* of the titular lemon. I never understood throwing away the lemon peel. It's free flavor, where all the essential oils reside with none of the acidity. Here it becomes a base for a simple sauce. You want to rely on the friction of stirring the pasta in the pot to make an emulsification between the lemon, the water, and the butter. But the cheese, which you add at the end, must be added off the heat, and should never be returned to it, lest the sauce breaks, the cheese coagulates and becomes oily.

Both the lemon squeezing and the emulsifying— a fancy word for stirring to suspend fat molecules in liquid molecules—at the end here are great steps for your kid to help with.

1. Bring a large pot of water to a boil and add the kosher salt until it's salty like the sea. Add the pasta and cook to 1 minute shy of al dente according to the package directions.

RECIPE CONTINUES

2. Meanwhile, in a large saucepan, melt the butter over medium-high heat, making sure not to allow it to brown. Add the lemon peel and stir until well coated. Remove from the heat.

3. Once the pasta is done, use tongs to add it directly to the pan with the butter. Reserve one cup (240ml) pasta water. Set the pan over high heat, add the reserved pasta water, and stir for 1 to 2 minutes, until it begins to look creamy.

4. Add the lemon juice and cook for another 1 minute. Remove from the heat. Add the parmesan and mix vigorously with a wooden spoon or spatula, working from the center out, until the sauce is emulsified, about 1 minute. Add more salt if desired.

5. Serve with more parmesan.

TAG RAGU

3 tablespoons extra-virgin olive oil, plus more for serving

2 garlic cloves, thinly sliced

3¼ cups (1½ pounds/700g) Ragu Bolognese (page 44)

½ cup kosher salt (70g), for the pasta water

1 pound (455g) fresh egg-noodle pasta, such as tagliatelle or pappardelle, homemade (page 99) or store-bought

Grated Pecorino Romano cheese, for serving

EQUIPMENT:

Rondeau

Another "Get dinner on the GD table" recipe, so keep the kids out of it. (But if they need something to keep them busy, let them grate cheese.)

This is a meltdown meal only if you've made your ragu ahead of time (which I recommend).

Make sure you pull the noodles out with enough time to let them cook with the ragu and don't be afraid to add pasta water to elongate the time in the pan.

Bolognese is not just a meat sauce. Its true expression is a very refined mixture of heavily seasoned ground beef (sometimes veal) with pork for added flavor, suffused with aromatics and a sliding scale of tomato. My traditional way of serving Bolognese is with an egg noodle, like a tagliatelle or pappardelle, or within a lasagna. I tend not to overcomplicate it.

1. If the ragu sauce is frozen, thaw it over medium heat in a rondeau. If it is not frozen, simply warm in the rondeau over medium heat.

2. In a large sauté pan, heat the olive oil over medium-high heat until it shimmers. Add the garlic and sauté until fragrant, about 1 minute. Add the ragu Bolognese, bring to a light simmer, and then turn down the heat.

3. Bring a large pot of water to a boil and add the kosher salt until it's salty like the sea. Add the pasta. For store-bought pasta, cook to 1 or 2 minutes shy of al dente according to the package directions. For homemade pasta, cook for around 3 minutes. Stir occasionally to prevent the pasta from sticking. Right before the pasta is done cooking, reserve ½ cup (120ml) pasta water.

4. Using tongs, pull the pasta out of the pot and directly into the pan with the sauce. Add the reserved pasta water. Increase the heat to medium-high and stir with a wooden spoon to emulsify the sauce with the pasta. Continue to do so for about 3 minutes, or until the sauce looks like it is sticking to the noodles.

5. Remove from the heat and sprinkle with some grated pecorino and a drizzle of olive oil. Serve immediately.

BASIL PESTO PASTA

FOR THE BASIL PESTO:

Kosher salt

5 bunches basil (6½ ounces/
190g), leaves picked

1 cup (250ml) extra-virgin olive
oil

Scant ½ cup (40g) walnuts

4 large garlic cloves, peeled but
whole

Pinch of chile flakes (optional)

6 tablespoons freshly grated
Parmigiano-Reggiano cheese

6 tablespoons freshly grated
Pecorino Romano cheese

FOR THE PASTA:

Kosher salt

1 pound fusilli, penne,
orecchiette, or trenette

1 tablespoon (10g) kosher salt

What makes a pesto a pesto isn't the basil. It's the combination of olive oil, nuts, and cheese pounded into a paste. (*Pesto* simply means "paste.") Genovese pesto, which uses basil with pine nuts, might be the most well known, but it's just one of many. A trapanese, for example, is a pesto made with tomato. As for me, I hate pine nuts. I hate the way they taste. I hate how expensive they are. So, I use walnuts. You can use whatever you want: walnuts, pine nuts, hazelnuts, pecans. It'll still be good. You can also experiment with the cheese. Here, as in Liguria, I use a mixture of pecorino and parmesan. If you like your pesto on the saltier side, use more pecorino. If you like it more mellow, lean on the parmesan.

Pesto will last up to 2 weeks in the fridge and 3 months in the freezer but I've never had it last more than a week. It's super versatile and can be eaten either hot or cold, folded into a pasta (or ribbons of zucchini for my low-carb friends), on a Pesto Grilled Chicken Sando (page 232), as an alternative to the pomo on the meatballs on page 149, or as a condiment for roasted vegetables. I often top it with some Save Your Ass Grilled Chicken (page 137).

1. **Make the basil pesto:** Prepare a bowl of ice water with 5 or 6 ice cubes and set it next to the stove. Bring a large pot of generously salted water to a rolling boil.

There's a lot of basil to work with here, from picking to blanching to wringing out. Appoint a keeper of the basil to help.

Blanching the basil sets the chlorophyll and prevents browning.

2. Add the basil and blanch for 30 seconds. Carefully move it to the ice bath with tongs. (Keep the pot of salted water on the stove, but not on the flame, for cooking the pasta. Turn the heat back on when you are ready to cook the pasta.)

3. Once the blanched basil is cooled, remove it from the ice bath and squeeze it out well with your hands. Place in a food processor. Reserve ½ cup (120ml) of ice water as well as the ice cubes.

4. In a small pot, combine ¼ cup (60ml) of the olive oil with the walnuts, garlic, and chile flakes (if using). Set over medium-low heat and toast until lightly browned and fragrant, with slight sizzling, about 10 minutes. Make sure this doesn't burn. Remove the pot from the heat. Using a fine-mesh sieve, drain the (deliciously infused) olive oil into a bowl and have at the ready.

5. Add the toasted garlic and walnuts to the food processor and turn on the machine. With the machine running, slowly add the reserved oil until emulsified. Once emulsified, turn off the food processor and add the ice cubes and reserved ice water. Blend well.

6. Once the food processor bowl is cold to the touch, add both cheeses and blend again. Add the salt and blend once more.

7. **Cook the pasta:** Return the salted water to boiling over medium high heat. Once boiling, add the pasta and cook to al dente according to the package directions. Drain the pasta and return to the pot. Fold in the basil pesto and kosher salt. Serve immediately.

FRESH PASTA DOUGH

3¼ cups (500g) tipo "00" flour, plus more for dusting

5 large eggs (300g total)

EQUIPMENT:

Bench knife, pasta maker (manual or stand mixer attachment)

If you need to get dinner on the table in 10 minutes or it's already been a stressful week, you don't need this smoke in your life. Make fresh pasta another day. It's fine. There's a false assumption in America that fresh pasta is superior to dried pasta from a high-quality producer. That is stupid. One is not better than the other. They're just different.

If today is not that day, avoiding the fresh pasta scene is not you failing to execute your cooking duties. Making fresh pasta is a luxury. Now that I've said that, it is also the most fun you can have with your kids. Think playing with Play-Doh, mix that with cooking, and then mix *that* all up with feeling like you are the most accomplished artist/human/parent in the world. That's the glorious feeling of making fresh pasta and feeding it to your family.

Pasta doughs come in two basic forms: those formed with water and those formed with egg, which is what we are making here. Egg dough is richer, softer, and more supple thanks to eggs, which hydrate more slowly because of the fat content. The softer dough, especially when made with a finer flour like tipo "00," allows for a pliable texture that can be mixed more rigorously. This creates a stronger gluten structure and more elasticity so it can be worked into more complex forms like ravioli or tortelli as well as standing up to heavier

RECIPE CONTINUES

sauces, as in a lasagna. Texturally it's what most Americans have come to know as ''fresh pasta'' and as such it is more of a crowd-pleaser than the more durable and chewy water-based doughs.

All of the steps can—and should—be done with your kid. Each is appealing in its own way, from whisking the eggs in the crater of flour to kneading the dough to running the pasta through the pasta maker into long perfectly (and imperfectly) formed sheets.

1. Pour the flour out onto a clean work surface. Using your hands, create a well with high walls in the middle of the flour.

2. Crack the eggs into the well. With a fork, whisk the eggs in their well, slowly starting to incorporate the flour into the egg until it looks like cake batter.

3. With a bench knife, push the unincorporated flour toward the center and chop the dough. Repeat until the dough begins to look shaggy.

4. Scrape the dough away from you to create one shaggy dough ball. When it comes together, knead the dough with your hands, incorporating any leftover flour.

5. Continue to knead the dough with the heel of your palm, folding the dough toward you and then simultaneously pushing and rolling it forward. Repeat this for about 5 minutes, until the dough feels smooth. If you press a finger into it, the dough should bounce back. Once this has been achieved, pinch the bottom of the dough ball together. Wrap in plastic and rest for 20 minutes on the counter.

6. Once unwrapped, the dough should be more supple and pliable. Knead it for 2 to 3 more minutes, until it becomes smooth again. Roll into a ball, pinch the creases on the bottom together. Rewrap the dough with plastic and let it rest for another 30 minutes.

7. After this final rest, your pasta will be ready to roll or you can store the dough in the refrigerator overnight. (If you are

RECIPE CONTINUES

rolling the pasta the next day, place the dough on the counter to bring it to room temperature for an hour before rolling it out.)

8. Dust a clean work surface with flour. Cut one-third of the dough from the ball, keeping the rest of the dough wrapped in plastic while working. Flatten the dough to the width of your pasta sheeter. Make sure there isn't any dry flour caked on it (this will result in the dough not passing through the pasta sheeter).

9. Set the pasta sheeter to the widest setting—usually 8—and feed one end of the dough through. Keep tension on both sides of the dough to make the pasta sheet taut until it completely passes through. Repeat again, decreasing the setting for each pass. It's important at this point to keep tension on the dough. Repeat until it's on the thinnest setting. If the sheet is too long to handle at once, simply cut it and run each sheet through the sheeter separately.

10. Once the pasta is sheeted, dust it with flour. Do not stack pasta sheets directly on top of one another, but rather stagger them. (This makes separating them much easier.) Repeat twice more with the remaining dough.

FOR LASAGNA:

1. Using the baking dish in which you'll be assembling the lasagna as a guide, measure the pasta dough, making sure it doesn't hang over the edge. Cut the rest of the sheets to match.

2. Prepare a sheet pan greased with olive oil. Bring a pot of generously salted water to a rolling boil. Gently lower 1 or 2 sheets of pasta into the pot of water and simmer for 30 seconds for each batch. Remove with tongs and lay on the prepared sheet pan, coating each piece with some olive oil to ensure they don't stick to one another. Reserve until you're ready to assemble the lasagna.

FOR TAGLIATELLE / FETTUCCINE / PAPPARDELLE:

1. Using the pasta sheeting attachment or a manual pasta maker, roll out the pasta into 8- to 12-inch (20 to 30cm) sheets. Allow them to dry on a cutting board, table, or rack set in a sheet pan for 10 to 15 minutes. Dust very lightly with flour.

RECIPE CONTINUES

2. Fold each sheet of pasta onto itself in thirds. Fold the ends to meet each other toward the center, then repeat again. Using a sharp knife, cut across the pasta roll into equal strips: ½ inch (13mm) wide for tagliatelle or fettucine and 1 inch (2.5cm) for pappardelle. Once cut, gently separate the strands.

3. Let the now cut noodles dry for another 10 minutes. Line a dry sheet pan with a paper towel. Separate the noodles into 4 small nests and place on the prepared tray. Cover the top with plastic wrap and refrigerate for up to 2 days. If freezing, place in the fridge first for 2 hours then in individual freezer bags. The pasta will last for up to 3 months in the freezer.

FOR RAVIOLI: *See Handmade Spinach and Cheese Ravioli (page 118)*

HANDMADE RICOTTA CAVATELLI

4⅔ cups (565g) tipo "00" flour

1⅓ cups (227g) semolina flour

3 tablespoons (28g) kosher salt, plus more for cooking the pasta

1½ pounds (680g) whole-milk ricotta cheese

2 eggs (120g total)

EQUIPMENT:

Stand mixer; bench knife; cavatelli machine, gnocchi or garganelli board (or really anything with ridges; e.g., a fork)

Making pasta by hand isn't hard. It just takes some time and practice. Among the homemade pasta doughs in this book, this recipe probably has the largest margin of error. That's thanks to the pliability of the dough and the magnanimity of the shape. Because of the ricotta, it's almost impossible to overwork. As for the shape—cavatelli, which comes from the word *cavare*, "to hollow"—the little dumplings are equally delicious if they're bigger or smaller or in funky shapes. And though you can make these on a cavatelli board (a small ridged cutting board, aka a gnocchi board), you can just as easily make them with a fork. Once made, cavatelli goes well with nearly any sauce, especially pesto (page 96)—which the ridges and cavity of the pasta are perfect for holding—though we often have it with a pork sausage ragu (see Cavatelli with Pork Sausage, page 110).

Making cavatelli is immensely fun, for your kids, for their cousins, for your kids' friends during playdates. It takes—or tolerates—a crowd. Don't overthink the size of the shapes. Because of the ricotta, they're forgiving in terms of cooking time.

1. In a stand mixer fitted with the whisk, whisk together both flours and the salt. Remove the whisk and connect the dough hook.

2. Add the ricotta and eggs, one at a time, mixing to incorporate after each addition. Set the mixer to the

RECIPE CONTINUES

lowest speed (called "stir" on some machines) and run for 4 minutes. Then increase the speed to low (level 2 on some machines) and beat for an additional 9 minutes.

3. Turn the dough out onto a clean well-floured surface. (Make sure to remove any dough from the dough hook and use that, too.) Knead the dough by hand for an additional 2 minutes, giving it a quarter-turn each time and folding the far end toward you, then pushing it away, fusing the top and bottom with the palm of your hand.

4. Once the dough is a smooth mass, tightly wrap it in plastic and rest it in the fridge for 30 minutes.

5. Lightly dust a sheet pan with tipo "00" flour and have nearby. Using a bench knife, cut a manageable piece— about one-eighth—of dough off the ball. Roll it into a rope roughly ½ inch (13mm) thick. Use the bench knife to cut the rope into ½-inch (13mm) segments. If you have a cavatelli board, flour it, and roll the segments away from you to form

cavatelli. (If you have a cavatelli board, you probably already know how to do this.) Or, use the back of a fork. Flour the fork and roll the segments away from you, using sufficient downward pressure to imprint ridges into the pasta. Place the cavatelli on the flour-dusted sheet pan as you work. Repeat with the remaining dough.

6. Bring a large pot of water to a boil and add ½ cup (70g) kosher salt until it's salty like the sea. Working in batches, add one-third of the cavatelli, stirring so they don't stick as they boil. Cover the pot and bring to a boil again for 2 minutes, until the cavatelli float to the surface. Using a spider strainer or a colander, remove the pasta, set aside, and continue until all the cavatelli have been cooked.

CAVATELLI WITH PORK SAUSAGE

Kosher salt

2 pounds (910g) Handmade
Ricotta Cavatelli (page 105)
or 1 pound (455g) dried pasta,
short cut

2 tablespoons extra-virgin olive
oil, plus more for drizzling

2 pounds (910g) pork sausage

12 ounces (340g) Broccoli di
Cicco, broccoli rabe, or broccoli,
chopped into 1-inch pieces

Thinly sliced peel and juice of
1 large lemon (30g)

3 cups (700ml) Pomodoro Sauce
(page 47)

1 to 2 teaspoons Calabrian chili
bomba (optional; see page 293)

Freshly grated Pecorino-Romano
cheese, for serving

With smaller florets and a
delicate flavor, Broccoli
di Cicco is easier to
incorporate into sauces and
thus easier eaten by the
possible broccoli skeptics.

A good recipe can expand or contract like an accordion. This cavatelli, for instance, can be a weekend activity, especially if you make the cavatelli yourself (see page 105). But when you're short on time, any other store-bought pasta, such as rigatoni or orecchiette, is just as good. (You'll want a short shape with plenty of nooks and crannies for the sauce to hide in.) Another easy modulation is the level of spice. Since the Calabrian chili bomba is added at the end, it's easy to personalize the level of spice for parents (more) or kids (less)—or leave it out entirely.

1. Bring a pot of generously salted water to a boil.

2. Working in batches, add one-third of the cavatelli, stirring so they don't stick together as they boil. Cover the pot and bring to a boil again for 2 minutes, until the cavatelli float to the surface. Using a spider strainer, remove pasta, set aside on a sheet pan, and continue until all the cavatelli have been cooked.

3. In a Dutch oven, heat the olive oil over high heat until it shimmers. Add the pork sausage and cook through, breaking it up with a wooden spoon. It should start to caramelize and the fat will render, 6 to 8 minutes, though it depends on the size of your pan.

4. Add the broccoli and lemon peel, stir, and cook for an additional 2 minutes. Add the pomodoro sauce and chili bomba (if using) and stir to combine. Add the cooked pasta to the sauce and stir to combine. Add the lemon juice. Remove from the heat and finish with a drizzle of olive oil and some pecorino.

ITALIAN SAUSAGE AND BROCCOLINI LASAGNA

PROJECT
COOKING

FOR THE RAGU:

⅓ cup (80ml) extra-virgin olive oil

1 medium red onion, thinly sliced

3½ pounds (1.6kg) sweet or spicy Italian sausage, casings removed

¾ cup (7 ounces/200g) tomato paste

2 (14-ounce/400g) cans crushed tomatoes

1 packed cup (40g) fresh basil leaves

2 pinches chile flakes (optional)

1 bunch broccolini (7 ounces/200g), cut into bite-sized pieces (2 cups)

FOR THE LASAGNA BUILD:

Fresh Pasta Dough (page 99)

2 teaspoons plus 2 tablespoons extra-virgin olive oil, plus more for the sheet pan

Kosher salt

4 bunches spinach (1½ pounds/ 700g), cut into bite-sized pieces

5 cups (6½ ounces/560g) packed grated low-moisture mozzarella cheese

Most pastas begin to deteriorate the moment they're made. Lasagna is the antithesis of that. I find it to be actually less good if you pull it out of the oven and go straight at it. It is exponentially better when it cools, congeals, and then is rewarmed. That secondary bake is key. I've done it a few ways. If you reheat it in the oven, you end up with a crispy crunchy lasagna; if you do it covered in the microwave, you get a soft supple ooey gooey one. You can't go wrong either way. It's just a matter of preference.

Most of the fun of making this with your kids is in the assembly. Who doesn't like a construction project?

In terms of eating, this single lasagna can last for a week or a month. I've cut the lasagna into portions, wrapped them in plastic wrap, and frozen them so when I need a quick—as in 10-minute— dinner, they are there eagerly awaiting use.

1. **Make the ragu:** In a rondeau, heat the olive oil over high heat until it shimmers. Add the onion and sauté for 30 seconds. Add the sausage and break up with a wooden spoon into medium-sized chunks. Render the fat and cook until the sausage is 60 to 70 percent done, about 5 minutes.

2. Stir in the tomato paste and cook for 1 to 2 minutes. Add the crushed tomatoes and stir. Add the basil and chile flakes

RECIPE AND INGREDIENTS CONTINUE

4 cups (30 ounces/850g) whole-milk ricotta cheese, lightly stirred

2 cups (220g) freshly grated Parmigiano-Reggiano cheese

EQUIPMENT:

Rondeau, pasta maker (manual or stand mixer attachment)

Don't want to make the lasagna sheets yourself? Fine. Store-bought lasagna sheets are totally cool, too.

(if using). Cook until the liquid reduces, about 30 minutes, stirring occasionally so the sauce doesn't scorch. The fat and olive oil will start to float to the surface, which means the water has cooked off and the tomato has become more concentrated.

3. Add the chopped broccolini to the ragu 10 minutes before the sauce is finished. Remove from the heat and cool.

Shhh! Hidden in these layers is an immense amount of spinach and broccolini.

4. Meanwhile, to build the lasagna: Make the pasta dough and roll out as directed. Using a 9 × 13-inch (23 × 33cm) baking dish as a guide, measure the pasta dough, making sure it doesn't hang too much over the edge. Cut the rest of the sheets to match. Or don't! (See Note.)

5. Prepare a sheet pan greased with olive oil. Bring a pot of generously salted water to a rolling boil. Gently lower 1 or 2 sheets of pasta into the pot of water and simmer for 30 seconds. Remove with tongs and lay on the oiled sheet pan, coating each piece with olive oil to ensure they don't stick to one another. Repeat for all the lasagna sheets.

6. Bring a generously salted pot of water to a rolling boil for the spinach. Prepare a bowl of ice water and set it next to the stove. Once the water is boiling, place the spinach in the pot with tongs and blanch for 30 seconds. Immediately remove and place in the ice bath. Wring out the spinach well with your hands and place in an empty bowl.

7. Position a rack in the center of the oven. Place a sheet pan on the bottom rack of the oven to catch any drips. Preheat a convection oven to 375°F (190°C) or a regular oven to 400°F (200°C).

8. Pour 2 teaspoons of the olive oil on the bottom of the baking dish. Lay 1 sheet of pasta flat along the bottom of

RECIPE CONTINUES

the dish. (It will cover only half.) Lay another sheet next to it, matching the seams in the middle of the dish. It's okay to patch it up with smaller pieces of pasta—no need for perfection here!

9. Spread 2 cups (470ml) of ragu evenly over the pasta in the baking dish. Add 1 cup (112 g) of mozzarella on top of the ragu.

10. Add another layer of 2 sheets of pasta (arranged as for the first layer and gently pressed down). Spread with 2 cups (425g) of the ricotta and top with ½ cup (100g) of the spinach, ⅓ cup (35g) parmesan, and ⅛ teaspoon salt.

11. Repeat the layering in this order: 2 sheets of pasta, ragu, mozzarella, another 2 sheets of pasta, ricotta, spinach, and parmesan until you are out of pasta. You'll end up with 3 ragu layers and 2 ricotta layers total (the last layer should be ragu).

12. On top of the last ragu layer, add 2 more sheets of pasta. Top with 2 cups (225g) mozzarella and ⅓ cup (75g) parmesan. Drizzle evenly with the remaining 2 tablespoons olive oil. Trim the edges of the pasta to fit the baking dish, leaving a little extra to create crispy edges.

NOTE: *If you have a lot of dough overhang, trim off the layers at the end of the lasagna with a sharp knife. Do not throw it out. Roll up the sheets and cut into thick noodles. You can cook these noodles in boiling water and serve with any leftover ragu for dinner, saving the lasagna for the day after. Or, you can add it to chicken soup or minestrone, cook it with some butter and cheese, or even fry it in olive oil and then scramble an egg in it. The important thing is not to throw it out but to use it.*

13. Brush a piece of parchment paper with olive oil and place it oiled-side down on top of the lasagna. Tightly cover the parchment in aluminum foil, two across widthwise and one lengthwise, to seal. Once wrapped, press down on the lasagna a final time.

14. Place lasagna on the middle rack and bake for 1½ hours.

15. Remove from the oven. If serving right away, remove the coverings and put the lasagna back into the oven for 25 more minutes or until the top has browned. If serving later, cool completely and cut into slices (see Storage at left).

PROJECT COOKING

HANDMADE SPINACH AND CHEESE RAVIOLI

FOR THE RAVIOLI:

Fresh Pasta Dough (page 99)

½ cup (120ml) extra-virgin olive oil

1½ pounds (680g) baby spinach, washed and well-dried (see Note)

Heavy pinch of kosher salt

15 ounces (425g) whole-milk ricotta cheese

½ cup (50g) freshly grated Parmigiano-Reggiano cheese

Egg wash: 1 egg, beaten

TO FINISH:

½ cup (70g) kosher salt

8 tablespoons (115g) unsalted butter

Freshly grated Parmigiano-Reggiano cheese, for serving

EQUIPMENT:

Pasta maker (manual or stand mixer attachment), rondeau, piping bag

In terms of time, effort, and equipment, this is the most ambitious recipe in the book. It's also the most fun. At my restaurant, Che Fico, my team makes some of the best pasta in the country: each raviolo, agnoletto, or mezza luna is painstakingly crafted. This is not that. It's not about perfection. It's about fun. I've included a delicious and luxurious brown butter sauce, but you can use Pomodoro Sauce (page 47) or Ragu Bolognese (page 44) as well.

1. Make the ravioli: Make the pasta dough as directed. Roll out 1 or 2 sheets, reserving the rest of the dough under a clean kitchen towel. Dust a dry sheet pan lightly with flour. Cut each sheet in half, lightly dust with flour, and lay on the prepared sheet pan, making sure not to overlap. It is better to keep the dough whole and roll out one or two at a time so you can save on space. Cover with plastic wrap.

Making ravioli is half fun family activity and half mealtime prep. Every single person has something to do: rolling sheets of pasta, filling it, shaping it, and, finally, eating it.

2. Heat a rondeau over high heat. Add the olive oil and once shimmering, add the spinach and salt and sauté for a few minutes, until wilted, working in batches, if needed. Remove the spinach from the pan, place in a bowl, and let cool completely.

RECIPE CONTINUES

3. Once the spinach has cooled, squeeze out all of the liquid you can with your hands. Finely chop the spinach and transfer it to a medium bowl.

4. Add the ricotta and parmesan to the spinach, mixing well until combined. With a rubber spatula, add the mixture to a piping bag and cut a hole in the tip about the size of a quarter. (If you don't have a piping bag, just use a small spoon to add the filling to the pasta.)

5. On a clean work surface, brush the excess flour off one pasta sheet and lay flat. Lightly brush one half of the pasta sheet horizontally with egg wash. On the egg-washed side, pipe (or spoon) filling in about 1½-tablespoon portions, spaced 2 fingers apart, in the middle of the egg-washed portion of the dough. The more consistent the spacing, the higher the yield of the ravioli.

6. Fold the other side of the pasta sheet on top of the egg-washed side. Using your fingers, press the dough together

around the filling, starting from the folded side out, making sure there isn't any air trapped in the center of the ravioli. You can also make a tiny incision with the tip of a knife, pushing the air out of the side and then resealing the dough. Repeat until all the ravioli are sealed.

7. Trim the raw edges of the pasta (not the folded side) lengthwise with a pizza cutter or sharp knife, leaving some space around the filling. Cut the ravioli into individual pieces. Place the finished ravioli on a floured tray.

8. Repeat, making two sheets at a time, until all the dough and ravioli filling has been used. (At this point, the filled ravioli can be frozen and cooked later.)

9. Bring a large pot of water to a boil and add the kosher salt until it's salty like the sea. Working in batches of 4 at a time (to avoid crowding the pot), add the ravioli to the boiling water and cook about 2 minutes, or until the ravioli floats.

RECIPE CONTINUES

NOTE: *You can use frozen cooked spinach instead. Just make sure it is fully thawed and the water squeezed out really well. You want the spinach to be as dry as possible.*

10. Meanwhile, in a sauté pan, melt 1 tablespoon of the butter until foaming and starting to slightly brown.

11. Use a slotted spoon to gently lift the first batch of ravioli directly from the boiling water into the pan and swirl the pasta around. Add a little pasta water if the ravioli stick and use a metal spatula to gently move them.

12. Cook the ravioli in the pan for 1 to 1½ minutes per batch. Allow the water and butter mixture to form a glaze around the ravioli, adding a couple of drops of pasta water if needed. Remove to a plate and continue with the remaining ravioli, adding another 1 tablespoon of butter each time a new batch of 4 ravioli hits the pan.

13. Place the ravioli onto a plate and spoon the butter sauce over them. Top generously with parmesan.

14. Repeat until all the ravioli has been made.

MEAT/FIS
POULTRY

ONE-DISH HALIBUT
WITH SUMMER
VEGETABLES,
page 128

IF YOU'VE HAD EVEN ONE MEAL AT MY HOUSE, YOU'VE heard me ask Helena to recite the most important part of the meal. "Protein!" she says. Protein it is. Whereas I may give some leeway with trying different vegetables, with protein, I don't. We finish the protein on our plate.

Because of that, and because no one wants an extended fight, these recipes are the ones that have met with the most success. The key is variation. Helena, and most kids, and hell, most humans, love everything fried. We don't have fried chicken (nuggets, Milanese, or "Jew-ish") all the time, but when we do, her face sheens with grease and joy. Helena isn't a frequent pescatarian, but when she *does* eat fish, which we started early, these recipes are what she favors; the ones that originally won her over. (The mild tasting halibut, in particular, is a great starter fish.)

The biggest help, I've found, with protein is unlocking the potential of ground meat. I always keep sausage or ground beef in the freezer. Unlike freezing a steak, freezing ground beef or pork or turkey doesn't change its texture. And when you need something fast, it's a lifesaver. It can become meatballs or meatloaf or chili or, in another context, a ragu.

ONE-DISH HALIBUT WITH SUMMER VEGETABLES

2 pounds (910g) halibut, cod, hake, or other white fish, skinned

Kosher salt and freshly ground black pepper

14 ounces (400g) fresh English peas

1 cup (100g) thinly sliced zucchini or other summer squash (from about 1 medium)

2½ ounces (75g) Padrón or shishito peppers (1 heaping cup), stemmed

7 ounces (200g) small tomatoes, such as Sungold or Sweet 100

20 fresh basil leaves (about ⅓ cup/6g)

⅓ cup (80ml) olive oil

Freshly ground black pepper

Juice of 1 large lemon

One thing I constantly hear from home cooks is that they wish they had more fish in their diets but they don't know how to go about it. Fish can be daunting, for sure. It's hard to know whether it's fresh. It's easy to overcook. But this is the most forgiving and accessible way to cook fish. I chose halibut because it's available on both the East and West Coasts but the recipe works just as well with hake or cod or other types of meaty fish. (Halibut is also not very oceanic, which makes it perfect for kids just dipping their toes into seafood.) Though I make this all the time for Helena, the genesis of this dish came from before she was born. I spent my entire life living in tiny apartments without great ventilation. Frying fish is less appealing when your bed is six feet away from the stove. When you bake it, on the other hand, there's no smell at all. And, frankly, there's hardly any work, which is what makes this a perfect recipe for holidays or dinner parties, when you don't want to spend the whole time cooking.

Popping peas out of their pods is an extremely satisfying task for a child. It's therapeutic for me, too.

Not only is halibut mild in flavor, but it's high in protein and niacin, as well as a good source of selenium, a trace mineral that helps maintain heart tissue.

RECIPE CONTINUES

1. Preheat the oven to 325°F (160°C).

2. Season the fish gently and evenly on both sides with salt and pepper and let sit for 15 to 20 minutes. (While the fish is sitting, prep all the vegetables.)

3. Place the fish in the center of a baking dish. Arrange the peas, zucchini, peppers, and tomatoes around the fish. Sprinkle half of the basil leaves on top of the fish and vegetables. Drizzle the olive oil over everything. Season the vegetables with a little extra salt, avoiding the fish. Add a few turns of black pepper over the entire dish and drizzle the lemon juice evenly over everything.

4. Bake uncovered until fish goes from opaque to white, about 30 minutes.

5. Finish with the remaining basil and serve.

SHRIMP FRA DIAVOLO

MELTDOWN MEAL

One 8-ounce (225g) leek

1½ pounds (700g) wild-caught Gulf shrimp (about 30), peeled and deveined

1 tablespoon (10g) kosher salt

½ cup (120ml) extra-virgin olive oil

3 tablespoons (45g) unsalted butter

½ cup (120ml) white wine

Thinly sliced peel and juice of 2 large lemons (¼ cup/60ml)

1 cup (285g) Arrabbiata Sauce (page 47)

1 bunch (3 ounces/80g) fresh Italian parsley, finely chopped

Pinch of chile flakes (optional)

EQUIPMENT:

Rondeau

Shrimp can be weird for kids. I think it has a lot to do with the fact that overcooked shrimp have an awful texture. A perfectly cooked shrimp should have a very subtle pop to the texture and should never be mushy. My tip for cooking shrimp is to have everything ready to go near the pan and work with high heat. Once the shrimp hit the pan you are on the clock. Unlike other proteins, shrimp tell you they are cooked by their color. So as soon as they turn pink or red, they need to get turned, and then they should come out of the pan.

If you want it less *diavolo*—meaning less spicy—use the regular pomo sauce instead of the arrabbiata.

If you want to see your kids laugh uncontrollably— or be horrified—get some shrimp with the heads on. When you remove them, use the heads as finger puppets à la *Good Morning, Vietnam*. It's actually hilarious. Unless you're a vegetarian. In which case I'm sorry for this whole thing.

1. Remove the outer, darker leaves of the leek. Trim roughly ½ inch (13mm) off the top and trim the bottom roots. Halve lengthwise and then thinly slice crosswise. Rinse the leeks well. Season the shrimp with the salt.

2. In a rondeau, heat the olive oil and butter over high heat, allowing the butter to brown slightly. Using tongs, add the shrimp to the pan in a single layer. Be sure not to overcrowd or overlap. As soon as they're layered, start flipping the

RECIPE CONTINUES

shrimp if they've started to develop color, starting with the first shrimp that went into the pan. (This happens very quickly.)

3. Once all the shrimp have been flipped, add the white wine, then the lemon peel. Add the sliced leeks and sauté, stirring, until aromatic, about 2 minutes. Stir in the lemon juice, then the arrabbiata sauce and parsley. Remove from the heat and add the chile flakes, if desired, for extra spice. Serve immediately.

CHICKEN NUGGETS À LA BABA GALINA

FOR THE CHICKEN:

⅓ cup (40g) all-purpose flour

1½ tablespoons (15g) kosher salt

1 teaspoon cracked black pepper

1 tablespoon onion powder

1 teaspoon garlic powder

1 teaspoon smoked paprika

1 teaspoon ground cumin

4 boneless, skinless chicken thighs, cut into bite-sized pieces

FOR THE BATTER:

1 cup (120g) all-purpose flour

1 cup (135g) cornstarch

1 tablespoon (10g) kosher salt

2 teaspoons (12g) baking soda

2 eggs (120g total), beaten

6 ice cubes

1¾ cups (420ml) sparkling water, cold

FOR FRYING:

1½ cups (680g) rendered chicken fat (schmaltz)

Growing up, my mother, Mama Galina, also known as Baba Galina, was adamant that my brother and I not stuff our bodies with highly processed food. If we wanted slushies from the corner store or roast beef from Safeway, she'd say, "Babychka, let's go home, I make it for you better." God bless her, but her homemade roast beef sandwiches and strawberry puree icees were never the same. As an adult, of course I applaud my mother. And as a parent, when Helena begs to go to McDonald's, I realize I've become my mother. "Let's make it at home, sweetie," I say. The difference between me and Galina is that I have the culinary chops to reverse-engineer the nuggets so they are actually better tasting and better for you. Instead of weird chicken mush, I use chicken thighs, so they're soft and tender. I drew from tempura for the battered, not breaded, nugget, made even lighter with the addition of sparkling water in the batter. By pressing the spices into the meat directly, and not mixing them into the batter, I make sure that each morsel bursts with flavor. And, most important, I use rendered chicken fat, or schmaltz, as the lipid for frying.

Hot oil can splatter but batter doesn't. Have your kid set up a batter station and help dip, but then bid them keep a safe distance as you fry.

RECIPE CONTINUES

1. **Prepare the chicken:** In a bowl, combine the flour, salt, pepper, onion powder, garlic powder, smoked paprika, and cumin. Add the chicken pieces and toss until evenly coated. Let sit for at least 15 minutes.

2. **Make the batter:** In a medium bowl, combine the flour, cornstarch, salt, baking soda, and beaten eggs. Add the ice cubes and sparkling water on top and whisk together until homogenous.

3. **Fry the chicken:** Line a plate with paper towels and set near the stove. Place the chicken fat in a Dutch oven and melt over medium-high heat, until it reaches around 375°F (190°C) on an instant-read thermometer.

4. With a pair of tongs, dip a seasoned chicken piece into the batter until well coated. Immediately place it into the pot of chicken fat. Repeat until you have one layer of chicken pieces, careful not to overcrowd (the pieces should not touch).

5. Fry until golden brown on one side, about 3 minutes. Flip to the other side and fry until cooked through, about another 3 minutes. These should be very crispy. If they're not quite crispy enough, fry on, my brother, fry on. Place the finished pieces of chicken on the paper towels. Repeat with the remaining chicken.

6. Serve hot with your preferred sauce(s).

SAVE YOUR ASS GRILLED CHICKEN

3 pounds (1.4kg) boneless, skinless chicken breasts (about 4 chicken breasts)

2 large garlic cloves, grated

2 tablespoons Dijon mustard

1 tablespoon extra-virgin olive oil

Grated zest and juice of 1 lemon (2 tablespoons/30g)

3 sprigs fresh thyme, leaves picked and chopped

2 sprigs fresh rosemary, leaves picked and chopped

¼ teaspoon smoked paprika

½ teaspoon ground cumin

1 tablespoon (9g) kosher salt

½ teaspoon freshly ground black pepper

Having some grilled chicken in the fridge is like having money in the bank. (We're big chicken eaters at my house.) Throughout the week I'll serve it with any of the salads, with sides like polenta, and with lighter pastas like Spaghetti al Limone (page 92), Spaghetti Aglio, Olio, e Pepperoncino (page 87), or Spaghetti Pomo (page 79).

Chicken breast gets a bad rap for being bland and flavorless. But the fault lies not in the breast but in the cook. Take a few minutes—literally just minutes—to make this simple marinade, and your chicken breasts will be juicy and piquant.

1. Slice the breasts in half on the horizontal, as if cutting a hamburger bun in half.

2. In a bowl, combine the garlic, mustard, oil, lemon zest, lemon juice, thyme, rosemary, smoked paprika, cumin, salt, and pepper. Mix well.

3. Add the chicken to the bowl and toss well. Marinate the chicken for 1 hour at room temperature. (If you're in a rush just do less time.)

4. Preheat the oven to 400°F (200°C).

5. Heat a grill or grill pan over high heat. Once the grill is hot, lay the chicken down and cook for 3 to 4 minutes per side, 2 to 3 minutes if they're the thinner side.

6. Let the chicken rest for 5 or 6 minutes. (You can refrigerate the chicken breasts at this point if you'd like, or if you are meal prepping.) Otherwise, allow to cool slightly.

SMOTHERED ITALIAN SAUSAGE

¼ cup (60ml) extra-virgin olive oil, plus more (optional) for serving

8 sweet Italian sausage links (2½ pounds/1.1kg)

3 red bell peppers, sliced

2 medium red onions, sliced

5 garlic cloves, sliced

1 bunch broccolini (2 cups/200g), ends trimmed and cut into 1-inch pieces

2 bunches spinach (4 ounces/115g total)

Chile flakes

1 (28-ounce/794g) can crushed tomatoes

1 bunch fresh basil (1½ ounces/45g), leaves picked

1 (12-ounce/355ml) jar mild banana peppers, undrained

Kosher salt and freshly ground black pepper

This is what I call a fridge-eater recipe. I made it one night with no time and no plan. I opened the fridge and grabbed everything that seemed at least vaguely to go together. I took some sausage from the freezer, some peppers on their last legs, some broccoli rabe, and a couple odds and ends of onions. Add to that the remnants of a few open cans of tomatoes and . . . voilà, classic sausage and peppers. The key here is getting a nice sear on the sausage and cooking the tomato down until it coats the sausage and vegetables well.

The longer this sits in the fridge, the more delicious it gets. Reheat it and then throw it on a hoagie or on a mound of mashed potatoes or with polenta.

1. In a Dutch oven, heat the olive oil over high heat until it shimmers. Add the sausages, cover, and cook until browned, 5 to 6 minutes. Flip and cook the other side.

2. Stir in the bell peppers, onions, and garlic, cover, and cook, stirring occasionally, until soft and fragrant, 5 to 6 minutes.

3. Add the broccolini and spinach, stir, cover, and cook, 3 to 4 minutes. Stir in the chile flakes and crushed tomatoes. Stir in the basil and banana peppers with their liquid. Cover and cook for 10 minutes, stirring occasionally.

4. Season with salt and pepper to taste. Finish with a drizzle of olive oil, if desired. Serve immediately.

MISO HONEY MUSTARD BAKED CHICKEN

FOR THE DRESSING/MARINADE:

6½ tablespoons (100g) Kewpie mayonnaise

2 tablespoons white miso

1½ tablespoons Dijon mustard

1 tablespoon honey

1 teaspoon (3g) kosher salt

Juice of ½ lemon
(1 tablespoon/15g)

FOR THE CHICKEN:

4 chicken leg quarters
(3 pounds/1.4kg total)

FOR THE SALAD:

½ small head (8 ounces/230g)
Savoy cabbage

Furikake, to finish

Toasted Sesame Seeds, to finish

Texture and flavor come together in this extremely easy to make chicken dinner. My inspiration was the simple salads you get as a side from Japanese takeout places plus, because it's dinner, baked chicken. The salad, made of chiffonade cabbage, is bright with texture and shapes. (The furikake, a Japanese seasoning powder made with sesame seeds, bonito, and nori, adds even more crunch.) But the time- and labor-saving shortcut here is to use the same marinade as a dressing, too. (See the Fennel and Calabrian Chili-Roasted Pork Rib Rack, page 157, for more marinade as sauce.) Ideally you make the marinade and let the chicken rest in it overnight, but when time is tight, 30 minutes will do the trick.

Can there be a better kitchen task than squirting mayonnaise from the squeeze bottle? Not for kids there isn't.

Miso, like many fermented foods, promotes gut health. White miso is the mildest of the misos and a great gateway to the umami-packed world of fermented soybeans.

1. **Make the dressing/marinade:** In a bowl, stir together the mayo, miso, mustard, honey, salt, and lemon juice until well combined. Measure out ½ cup (120g) of the mixture for the marinade and refrigerate the remainder for the dressing.

2. Toss the chicken in the marinade and refrigerate, covered, for at least 30 minutes and up to overnight.

3. When ready to cook, preheat the oven to 375°F (190°C). Line a sheet pan with aluminum foil. Place a wire rack over the lined tray.

4. Arrange the chicken on the rack and roast for 45 minutes.

5. **Meanwhile, make the salad:** Remove the core of the cabbage by cutting a V into the base. Cut into quarters and then, with a sharp knife, very thinly slice the cabbage from top to bottom. The cabbage should look like frizzy angel hair.

6. Place the cabbage in a small bowl. Drizzle the desired amount of reserved dressing over it. Finish with furikake or toasted sesame seeds.

7. Remove the chicken and let rest for 5 minutes. Drizzle the remaining dressing over the baked chicken.

8. Serve the chicken and the salad together.

CHICKEN (OR ANYTHING) MILANESE

2 cups (240g) all-purpose flour

1 heaping tablespoon fresh thyme leaves, chopped

1 heaping tablespoon fresh oregano leaves, chopped

1½ heaping tablespoons fresh Italian parsley leaves, chopped

2 tablespoons (20g) kosher salt, plus more for serving

¼ teaspoon freshly ground black pepper

2 cups (225g) fine dried bread crumbs

4 large eggs, whisked well

4 boneless, skinless chicken breasts (about 12 ounces/ 340g each)

½ cup (120ml) extra-virgin olive oil, plus more as needed

2 tablespoons (30g) unsalted butter, plus more as needed

1 lemon, cut into wedges

EQUIPMENT:

Rondeau

Pounding chicken breasts is a good way to use up excess energy, both yours and your kids'. (You can also just butterfly them or use mini-cutlets.)

For a long time, I didn't properly respect Milanese. It's a fried chicken cutlet, how exceptional could it be? But I now realize I was wrong and I apologize. Fine Milanese—no matter whether chicken, veal, or pork—is an art form. By pounding (or slicing) the meat thin, being generous with the herbs, and being even more generous with the butter, Milanese is not only good, it's exceptional. It's satisfying and pleasing and flavorful, a song of crisp coating and juicy inside. Nothing more needs to be done with it, but I like to serve this to Helena with a simple salad.

1. Set up a breading station with three shallow dishes: Spread enough flour in a large shallow dish to cover it entirely. In a second dish, mix together the herbs, salt, pepper, and bread crumbs. Place the beaten eggs in the third.

2. Butterfly the chicken by trimming any cartilage or extra pieces off the breast meat. Lay the chicken breast on a work surface, with the thicker part of the breast facing the right (or facing left if you're left-handed). Using a sharp knife, slice through the thickest part of the breast on the horizontal (like splitting a hamburger bun), but do not cut all the way through. When you open up the butterflied breast it should be heart-shaped. Repeat with the remaining chicken.

RECIPE CONTINUES

3. Spread a large piece of plastic wrap on the work surface. Drizzle ½ teaspoon of the olive oil over the plastic. Lay a butterflied breast on one half. Drizzle another ½ teaspoon olive oil on the top half of the plastic and fold it over the chicken so it is completely covered. With a mallet or a heavy-bottomed pot, pound out the breast, making sure to make contact only with the flat part of whatever you're using until the chicken is ¼ inch (6mm) thick. Once done, you can restructure/shape the pounded chicken back into a heart shape. Repeat with the rest of the breast pieces, replenishing the olive oil if needed. If the chicken peeks out of the plastic while pounding, just push it back in.

4. Set up two sheet pans each with a wire rack. Set one near the breading station and one near the stove.

5. Lightly dredge a cutlet in the flour, coating both sides. Dust off excess. Dip it in the eggs, coating both sides, and shaking off the excess. Finally, dip the cutlet in bread crumbs, making sure to press them into the cutlet so that it is well coated. Set on the rack in the sheet pan. Repeat with the remaining cutlets.

6. In a rondeau, combine the olive oil and butter and heat over high heat. Once the butter melts and stops foaming, reduce the heat to medium and carefully place one piece of chicken in the pan. Carefully swirl the pan. It should be actively bubbling but never smoking and the oil should never darken. Cook the cutlet for about 2 minutes. Flip carefully with tongs and cook the other side for about 2 minutes. Remove the fried cutlet with tongs and lay on the rack-lined sheet pan.

7. Repeat with the rest of the cutlets. If you notice the fat is low, add an additional ¼ cup (60ml) of oil and 1 tablespoon of butter and bring it back up to temperature before continuing.

8. Season with a small pinch of salt and serve immediately with lemon wedges.

A 100% CHANCE OF MEATBALLS

¼ cup (60ml) extra-virgin olive oil, plus more for greasing

1 pound (455g) lean ground beef (90/10)

1 pound (455g) ground pork

1 large garlic clove, grated

¼ small yellow onion, finely diced

4 sprigs fresh thyme, leaves picked and chopped

2 sprigs fresh rosemary, leaves picked and chopped

2 sprigs fresh oregano, leaves picked and chopped

½ cup (35g) chopped fresh Italian parsley

Pinch of chile flakes

½ cup (40g) freshly grated Parmigiano-Reggiano cheese

2 large eggs

1 tablespoon (10g) kosher salt

⅓ cup (35g) fine dried bread crumbs

1 cup (250ml) whole milk

A full batch (6 quarts/5.7L) Pomodoro Sauce (page 47)

EQUIPMENT:

#10 (3-ounce) ice cream scoop, rondeau, digital kitchen scale

When Niko, the twelve-year-old son of my then-girlfriend Vanessa, started staying with us, he was a tough nut to crack. I get it. He didn't know me and I didn't know him and now he was living in my house, under my rules. It was a challenge to get him to openly admit he liked anything. And trust me, I tried. It wasn't until I made him spaghetti and meatballs that he smiled. It was a small one, slight and still guarded, but the first smile on record at his new home. Now, when it's meatball night, he helps me peel garlic and form the meatballs. Whether they're on spaghetti or in a sandwich, the meatballs are at home in Pomodoro Sauce (page 47) just like Niko is at our house.

Meat-scrunching! Hand-mixing! Ball-forming! Meatball making is heaven for a tactile kid.

1. Preheat the oven to 425°F (220°C). Line a sheet pan with aluminum foil and lightly grease it with olive oil.

2. In a large bowl, combine the beef, pork, garlic, onion, herbs, chile flakes, parmesan, eggs, salt, and ¼ cup (60ml) olive oil.

3. In a small bowl, soak the bread crumbs in the milk until well absorbed, about 5 minutes.

4. Fold the soaked bread crumbs into the meat mixture. Mix vigorously with your hands for about 30 seconds until well combined. The mixture will be very wet.

RECIPE CONTINUES

5. Using a #10 (3-ounce) ice cream scoop, form meatballs and place them on the lined pan. (If you don't have an ice cream scoop, weigh out 3-ounce/85g portions on a kitchen scale and with hands greased with olive oil, form into balls.)

6. Bake the meatballs until golden brown, about 40 minutes.

7. Meanwhile, in a rondeau, gently heat the pomodoro sauce over medium heat until it is hot, stirring occasionally.

8. Remove the meatballs from the oven and, with a spatula or tongs, carefully place them in the warmed sauce. Cook on low heat for an additional 10 minutes.

SPAGHETTI AND MEATBALLS

Kosher salt

1 pound (455g) spaghetti

8 meatballs (from A 100% Chance of Meatballs, page 146), baked but not in sauce

3 cups (700ml) Pomodoro Sauce (page 47)

1 cup (110g) freshly grated Parmigiano-Reggiano cheese, for serving

¼ cup (60ml) olive oil, for serving

½ cup (25g) fresh basil leaves, for serving

EQUIPMENT:

Rondeau

Hits the spot for every family. I've never seen my kids consume more protein than when they're crushing meatballs. It's the perfect amount of family togetherness and as far as doing projects together it's ideal. Bulletproof. The most amount of action from and requested.

1. Bring a large pot of water to a boil and add ½ cup (70g) salt until it tastes salty like the sea. Add the pasta and cook to 1 minute shy of al dente according to the package directions.

2. While the pasta is cooking, in a rondeau, combine the pomodoro sauce and meatballs and bring to a boil over medium-high heat. Reduce to a simmer and hold warm until the pasta is ready.

3. Drain the pasta in a colander and toss with the meatballs and pomodoro until well coated.

4. Serve with parmesan, olive oil, and fresh basil.

MEATBALL HERO

2 soft bread rolls, hero or sausage rolls

6 meatballs (from A 100% Chance of Meatballs, page 146), baked but not in sauce

1 cup (250ml) Pomodoro Sauce (page 47)

6 slices provolone cheese (6 ounces/170g total)

1 ounce (30g) Parmigiano-Reggiano cheese, grated

Pickled peppers (optional)

Meatballs and spaghetti is a classic; a meatball hero might be even better. This isn't one of those things to get fancy with. You don't want a crusty bread. You want a soft squishy roll that tastes like you got it at Subway. A soft roll means you're not going to exert undue pressure on the meatballs, which might cause them to squish or, worse, shoot out from the back of the bun. Don't sleep on the pickled peppers either. This is a rich sandwich, so the peppers, with their shot of acid and crunch, are key to its balance.

1. Preheat the oven to 400°F (200°C). Slice the rolls open without cutting all the way through.

2. In a pot, combine the meatballs and sauce, cover, and simmer over low heat. (If you don't have enough sauce to cover the meatballs at least halfway, add 2 tablespoons of water and let it cook off.) You can also microwave them, but make sure you cover the container to avoid splatters.

3. Spoon the hot meatballs in sauce onto the bottom half of each roll. Add extra sauce on top. Set 3 slices of the provolone on top of the meatballs in each sandwich and sprinkle the parmesan on top of that.

4. Bake the sandwiches open-faced in the oven until the cheese is melted.

5. Remove from the oven. If using, add the pickled peppers on top of the melted cheese, and serve.

"JEW-ISH" FRIED CHICKEN

FOR THE MARINATED CHICKEN:

1 whole chicken
(3 to 3½ pounds/1.4 to 1.6kg)

1 cup (250ml) buttermilk

2 tablespoons (18g) kosher salt

1 tablespoon smoked paprika

1½ teaspoons garlic powder

1½ teaspoons onion powder

¼ teaspoon ground cumin

1 teaspoon coarsely ground
black pepper

FOR THE BREADING:

¾ cup (90g) all-purpose or
whole wheat flour

¾ cup (90g) cornstarch

1 teaspoon garlic powder

1 teaspoon onion powder

½ teaspoon ground cumin

1 teaspoon smoked paprika

2 teaspoons kosher salt

½ teaspoon coarsely ground
black pepper

3 pieces matzo, finely crumbled

This recipe was passed down to me by generations of grandmothers, from the shtetls of the Pale of Settlement to modern-day California. In it is all the suffering and peregrinations of the Jewish people . . . Just kidding. I made this up for the book. I wanted to include a recipe for fried chicken, a wonderful at-home technique, and, simultaneously, wanted to add something to the discourse. There are plenty of very good recipes out there. What would make mine special? At first I tried to make a healthy fried chicken, using olive oil to fry the bird. It was too expensive and the chicken too dark. Then I looked around in my pantry, perpetually full of leftover matzo from Passover. Leaning into my Ashkenazi background, I came up with this recipe. The secret is in the lipid. I use schmaltz, the king fat of the Jewish kitchen. The first bite of this schmaltz-fried matzo-coated chicken filled my mouth with what I can only describe as exponential chicken flavor. Set off with a drizzle of honey and the benediction of Crystal hot sauce, it's an undeniable winner. Golden, succulent, intensely flavorful, whether or not she ever made it, this chicken would fill my grandmother with *naches*.

To make this a whole lot faster—or if you just don't love breaking down a chicken—get the equivalent weight in thighs and drumsticks.

RECIPE AND INGREDIENTS CONTINUE

24 ounces (680g) rendered
chicken fat (schmaltz)

TO FINISH:

Kosher salt (optional)

Hot sauce, for serving

Honey, for serving

1. **Marinate the chicken:** Break the chicken down into thighs, drumsticks, wings, and breasts. Cut the breasts in half on a diagonal.

2. In a large bowl, mix together the buttermilk, salt, smoked paprika, garlic powder, onion powder, cumin, and pepper. Add the chicken and mix until all the pieces are coated.

3. Transfer the chicken to a 1-gallon (4L) freezer bag and scrape the rest of the marinade into the bag. Remove as much air as possible before sealing the bag. (Use a vacuum sealer if you have one.) Refrigerate for at least 6 hours and up to 24 hours. (You can also just leave the chicken in the bowl, push it down until compact, and cover it with plastic wrap, making sure the plastic wrap is in contact with the entire surface area of the chicken.)

4. Remove the chicken from the refrigerator and let it come to room temperature, about 1 hour.

5. Meanwhile, preheat the oven to 350°F (180°C).

6. **When ready to fry, make the breading:** In a shallow dish, mix together the flour, cornstarch, garlic powder, onion

- *When handling chicken, abide by the saying "one dirty hand, one clean hand." Use one hand to handle chicken when wet and keep the other free and clean, even if you wear gloves, for the inevitable need to pick up your phone or grab your kid an applesauce at the exact moment you decide to bread chicken, #IYKYK.*

- *If you're like most people in America and only have one sheet pan in your kitchen, reserve half of the tray for the raw breaded chicken and leave the other half clean, so you have a landing pad for the finished fried chicken.*

powder, cumin, smoked paprika, salt, pepper, and matzo, making sure all the spices are evenly distributed.

7. Set up a breading station: Line a sheet pan with a wire rack. Working with one piece at a time (see Notes), add the chicken to the dry mixture, pressing the chicken into the dredge, making sure to coat the entire surface. Place each finished piece on the rack.

8. Place a clean wire rack in another sheet pan (see Notes) and set near the stove. In an 8-quart (8L) pot, add enough chicken fat to fully submerge the pieces of chicken and spread them in a single layer without touching one another. Heat over high until a deep-fry thermometer reads 325°F (163°C). (If you don't have a thermometer, carefully place a small piece of excess chicken into the oil. If it sizzles, it's ready.) It is important to let the water cook off from the chicken fat before adding chicken pieces or they will stick to the bottom.

9. Using tongs, gently place a few pieces of chicken in the fat (no more than a single layer). To avoid splatter, do not drop them into the pot, lay them away from you. Fry the chicken pieces until golden brown, 4 to 5 minutes on each side. When finished, place on the wire rack in the sheet pan.

10. Once all the chicken pieces have been browned, place the sheet pan in the preheated oven to finish cooking, until an instant-read thermometer reads 160° to 170°F (71° to 77°C) for breast pieces and over 170°F (77°C) for leg pieces, 10 to 14 minutes.

11. Remove the chicken from the oven and let rest for 5 minutes. Season with more salt to taste. Serve with hot sauce and honey.

STORAGE: Allow to cool, then store in an airtight container in the refrigerator for up to 1 week. It's delicious cold or reheat it in the oven at 375°F (190°C) for 20 minutes.

FENNEL AND CALABRIAN CHILI-ROASTED PORK RIB RACK

WEEKNIGHT MEAL

One 4-rib pork rack (2½ to 3 pounds/1.1 to 1.4kg)

FOR THE MARINADE:

2 tablespoons Calabrian chili bomba (see page 293) or Calabrian chili spread

Grated zest and juice of 1 large lemon

2 tablespoons extra-virgin olive oil

2 tablespoons honey

1 sprig rosemary, leaves picked and chopped

1½ teaspoons fennel pollen or fennel seeds

2 tablespoons (20g) kosher salt

TO FINISH:

Extra-virgin olive oil

Coarse sea salt

Fennel pollen (optional)

A lot of us have had a similar experience growing up with pork chops: They're either breaded and fried, with a substantial amount of greasiness, or they're so overcooked they come out drier than a drought. But if you find a source for responsibly raised delicious pork, then that doesn't have to be the case. And it's worth the added expense and effort. Unlike in meatloaf or ground beef or Italian sausage, things where you're adding extra flavor, there's nothing to hide behind in a pork chop. Quality translates into flavor, which, in the best cases, can be nutty and unctuous. And if you trust your pork, you can cook it properly; that is, slightly pink and very juicy. That's especially true when you're cooking a rack—as opposed to individual chops—which helps to retain that juiciness.

1. Dry the pork rack well with paper towels. Crosshatch and score the fat cap with a paring knife.

2. Meanwhile, make the marinade: In a bowl, stir together the chili bomba or chili spread, lemon zest, lemon juice, oil, honey, rosemary, fennel, and salt.

3. Place the pork in a freezer bag and pour in the marinade, coating the pork well. Seal, removing the air from the bag. Marinate overnight in the fridge.

RECIPE CONTINUES

4. When ready to cook, cover a sheet pan with foil and place a wire rack on top. Carefully remove the pork from the marinade and place the meat on the rack, fat-side up. Reserve the marinade and place in a small saucepot. Allow the pork to come to room temperature for 1 hour.

5. Meanwhile, preheat the oven to 350°F (180°C).

6. Transfer the pork to the oven and cook for 20 minutes.

7. Meanwhile, bring the marinade to a boil over medium-high heat for 90 seconds. (Boiling renders the marinade safe to consume.) Remove from the heat and have at the ready.

8. Using a silicone brush, glaze the pork rack with some of the reduced marinade. Return the pork to the oven and bake for another 20 minutes.

9. Remove from the oven and brush with marinade again. Return to the oven and cook until the internal temperature reaches 145°F (63°C), about another 20 minutes. The total cooking time will be roughly 50 to 60 minutes.

10. Let the pork rest for 15 minutes before serving.

11. To serve, slice the bottom of the pork rack straight down, following the line of the ribs, slicing evenly. Brush with more marinade, drizzle with olive oil, and sprinkle with coarse sea salt and fennel pollen (if using).

NOTES:

- This recipe can be easily expanded to accommodate a larger pork rack. Just double all the ingredients. The method stays the same.

- If you can only find individual pork chops, marinate them the same way, then cook them in a grill pan over medium-high heat for 4 minutes a side. If they're thick, finish them in the oven at 350°F (180°C) for 6 minutes.

CRISPY SKIN PAN-ROASTED SALMON WITH TOMATO BASIL RELISH

FOR THE SALMON:

2½ to 3 pounds (1.1 to 1.4kg) salmon fillet

Kosher salt and freshly ground black pepper

Extra-virgin olive oil

FOR THE RELISH:

⅓ cup (80ml) extra-virgin olive oil

4 large garlic cloves, sliced

2 cups (14 ounces/400g) Sungold tomatoes

½ cup (12g) packed fresh basil leaves

1 tablespoon (15g) coarse sea salt

¼ cup (60ml) red wine vinegar

The key to cooking all proteins is understanding their size, their density, how long it takes to cook them, and what texture you're trying to achieve. If you want fish with a crispy skin, you want to avoid steaming it in the pan. One way to do this is to make sure that the skin is super dry and very clean. Salting the fish early, as I do here, pulls moisture out of the skin. Let the fish come to room temperature before you cook—in fact, you should let all your proteins come to room temperature before you cook—as this ensures an even cook. Make sure your pan and oil are hot enough and, once the salmon is in the pan, press down to make sure there are no air bubbles underneath it. Then listen. The fish should sizzle, not bubble. And if it starts to sizzle too much, reduce the heat a little. The idea here is to lightly fry the fish, not char it to oblivion. Done right, this is flavorful but not fishy, with a wonderfully tender meat and a crispy skin that will win over even the most fish-avoidant kid.

Omega-3 fatty acids, which are abundant in salmon, are particularly helpful for the development of children's brains, nerves, and vision.

1. Preheat the oven to 325°F (160°C).

2. Lay the salmon on a paper towel, skin-side up. Scrape the salmon skin against the grain with a knife to ensure that all the scales are off and to remove any schmutz.

RECIPE CONTINUES

3. Flip the salmon over and lay it on a cutting board. With a clean knife, slice the salmon fillet into even 2- to 3-inch (5 to 7.5cm) pieces. Wipe the knife clean on a clean kitchen towel.

4. Line a sheet pan with paper towels. Lay the cut salmon on it, skin-side up. Salt the salmon skins evenly, from high above the fish. This will pull extra moisture from the skin to ensure crispiness. Let sit for 10 to 15 minutes.

5. Pat the skin of the salmon completely dry with a paper towel. Take the paper towels out of the sheet pan and replace with a wire rack. Flip the fillets over and place on the rack, skin-side down. Salt lightly again and add pepper to taste. Flip the salmon skin-side up again and lightly coat with olive oil with your fingers.

6. Heat a large sauté pan over high heat with enough olive oil to coat the bottom without pooling. Once the oil is shimmering, lay a piece of salmon skin-side down in the pan, bending the sides of the fillet gently upward and placing the center of the fillet down first. Then lay down the sides. This prevents air pockets and creates an even cooking surface. Cook for 2 to 3 minutes.

7. Once you hear the fish start to sizzle, not bubble, you can turn the heat down to medium (nice medium heat allows the skin to become crispy). Pinch the uncooked side and slide a fish spatula under to check skin crispiness. If a spot needs to crisp more, lay it back down and press the fish down on that spot. Flip the fish and cook for another 3 minutes.

8. Place the cooked salmon on the sheet pan lined with a wire rack. Repeat with the remaining salmon.

9. Once all the skin is crisped, transfer the fillets to the oven and bake for an additional 3 to 5 minutes, depending on the thickness of the salmon.

10. **Meanwhile, make the relish:** Heat a sauté pan over high heat. Add the olive oil and when hot, add the garlic and sauté until slightly golden brown, about 1 minute. Add the tomatoes and stir and toss to coat the tomatoes. Add the basil leaves and stir and cook until the basil has wilted and the tomatoes are just starting to burst open, about 5 minutes.

11. Remove from the heat and stir in the sea salt and vinegar.

12. Pour the relish over the salmon to finish, and serve.

HOMEMADE CHEESEBURGERS!

2 pounds (910g) ground beef (80/20)

¼ cup (60g) Dijon mustard

1 cup (220g) mayonnaise

2 thin slices red onion, cut crosswise, rings popped out

4 (½-inch/13mm) slices heirloom tomato (only if in season)

8 slices sharp cheddar cheese, or whatever cheese you prefer

1 head iceberg lettuce, torn into small wedges, with the leaves separated

2 dill pickles, very thinly sliced

Coarse sea salt

Freshly ground black pepper

3½ tablespoons (50g) unsalted butter, plus more if needed

4 burger buns, split open

Kosher salt

Building a burger is both fun and an opportunity for your child to build their own sense of self (and discover the principles of structural engineering).

You might ask, why make a burger at home at all? The simple answer is: It's satisfying. Sure, it's a project. Sure, it's easier to just head to the drive-through. But having your kids eat something that you've made—especially if it rivals their favorite burger chain (in my case, In-N-Out)—gives them a sense of where real food comes from.

1. Remove the meat from the refrigerator at least 30 minutes before cooking.

2. Preheat the oven to 375°F (190°C).

3. Divide the meat into 4 equal portions. Place a cutting board on a work surface. Throw each burger onto the cutting board with force (see Note). Repeat this until the meat becomes tacky. Form the burgers into even round patties, roughly 5 inches (13cm) in diameter and no thicker than ½ inch (13mm). If they are any thicker, once they start cooking, the meat will contract and the patty will become thicker. Place on a sheet pan and set aside at room temperature.

4. In a small bowl, whisk together the mustard and mayonnaise to make a Dijonnaise.

5. Set out the burger components on separate plates: the onion, cheddar, tomatoes (if using), lettuce, and pickles. Season the tomatoes with sea salt and black pepper.

RECIPE CONTINUES

6. In a large sauté pan, melt the butter over medium-high heat. Once it stops foaming, add the burger buns, cut-side down, and toast quickly, pressing down lightly on the buns to make sure the entire surface area gets buttered. If you need to add more butter to toast, add an additional tablespoon. Remove the buns and set aside on a sheet pan, tops on one side, bottoms on the other.

7. Season the burgers with kosher salt and black pepper, edge to edge. Press the seasoning into the patties. Flip the patties and season with more salt and pepper; pressing them in as well.

8. Spread Dijonnaise on both sides of each bun, covering the entire surface area. Arrange the pickles on the bottom buns, in one layer, without any gaps. Place the tomato slices (if using) on top of the pickles. Add 2 or 3 thin onion rings on top of the tomato.

9. Wipe out the sauté pan you just used for the buns. Turn the heat on high. Add 2 tablespoons butter and melt. Once the butter has stopped foaming and starts to brown lightly, add the burger patties to the pan. Depending on the size of the sauté pan, you might have to work in batches. It is important not to crowd the pan. Press the burgers down with force to ensure that the centers don't have any air bubbles beneath them and don't contract too much. After pressing, let the patties cook over high heat. Don't move the burgers after smashing.

10. After about 2½ minutes, give the burgers one more press and cook for 30 more seconds. Carefully flip the burgers. The cooked sides should be very caramelized and have a nice crust on them. Do not press the burgers again. Add 2 cheese slices onto the cooked sides. Cook for about 2 minutes. Remove the patties from the pan and place on a sheet pan. Repeat with the rest of the patties.

NOTE: *Throwing the patties agitates the meat and creates myosin, a protein that causes muscle contraction. It's important for burger making, as myosin binds fat and water to the meat, leading to a more tender burger. When you agitate ground meat, it becomes a little tacky, allowing it to stick together. You don't want to overmix it, but you do want it to adhere. This is good to know when making meatloaf, burgers, or anything else with ground meat. A literal rule of thumb: You should be able to form a ball of meat, stick your thumb through it, and hold it without the meat falling off your finger.*

11. After you've cooked all the burgers, move the sheet pan to the oven and roast for 1½ minutes.

12. Place the patties on the prepared bottom buns. Place several iceberg slices on top of each patty. Top with the reserved burger buns, press down gently, and serve immediately.

PORK CARNITAS

FOR THE MARINADE:

3 tablespoons (30g) kosher salt

2 large oranges, peeled and pulped

1 head garlic, cloves smashed and peeled, peels reserved

1 yellow onion, sliced

½ cinnamon stick, broken

2 tablespoons chili powder

½ teaspoon freshly ground black pepper

6 fresh bay leaves

FOR THE PORK:

5 pounds (2.3kg) boneless pork shoulder, cut into large chunks

1¾ cups (14 ounces/400g) lard

2 (12-ounce/350ml) bottles Negro Modelo or other dark lager

1 cup (250ml) whole milk

Generous ⅓ cup (70g) packed dark brown sugar

FOR SERVING:

Corn tortillas, warmed

Diced white onion

Chopped fresh cilantro

Lime wedges

Salsas

Unlike most stagiaires (kitchen interns) who work their way through the kitchens of Europe at the beginning of their careers, I didn't start staging until after I had already been cooking in professional kitchens for years. So, unlike most stagiaires, who were looked at as liabilities, I was given a certain amount of latitude. One measure of their respect was that the chefs frequently asked me to make family meal. That's where these carnitas come in. As an American-born kid growing up in a Russian household I found my happy place in Mexican and Chinese restaurants. And during my time in Europe, I craved carnitas all the time. After I had Helena, those restaurant family meals provided inspiration for real family meals. These days we have taco parties with carnitas at least once a month. And if we have leftovers, even better; carnitas are like a confit in that once you cook them, they can stay in their fat for a while in the fridge, getting better with each reheat.

Dragons love taco parties. So do kids. Once the carnitas are simmering, go off and do something else. Reassemble for a make-it-yourself taco party (and story time).

1. **Make the marinade:** In a bowl, combine the salt, the orange peel and pulp, garlic cloves, onion slices, cinnamon stick, chili powder, black pepper, and bay leaves.

2. **Prepare the pork:** Add the pork pieces to the marinade and toss to coat well. Place the pork and marinade in a

1-gallon (4L) freezer bag, seal, and marinate overnight in the refrigerator.

3. An hour before cooking, remove the pork from the refrigerator and let it come to room temperature.

4. In a large Dutch oven or rondeau, melt the lard over high heat. Carefully add the pork pieces and brown on all sides, reserving any excess marinade. Timing will vary, depending on the size of the vessel among other things, so just make sure the pork is golden brown on all sides.

5. Add the beer to deglaze, scraping the bottom of the pot with a wooden spoon. Then add the milk, brown sugar, and any of the leftover marinade juices and solids to the pot. Bring to a lively simmer over medium-high heat. Once it starts to simmer, drop to low heat and cook, uncovered, until tender, about 2 hours.

6. Let the pork rest in the lard for 45 minutes before serving.

7. Serve with warm corn tortillas, onion, cilantro, lime wedges, your favorite salsas, and an ice-cold beer (for you) and milk (for the kids).

PORK CARNITAS,
page 168

THE BEST FRICKING MEATLOAF IN THE WORLD

PROJECT COOKING

FOR THE MEATLOAF:

8 ounces (225g) bacon, finely chopped

1 medium yellow onion, finely diced

5 garlic cloves, finely chopped

2½ pounds (1.1kg) lean ground beef (90/10)

⅓ cup (90g) ketchup

3 large eggs

1¼ cups (130g) bread crumbs

1 cup (80g) packed fresh parsley, picked and chopped

⅓ cup (80ml) whole milk

4 teaspoons (13g) kosher salt

1 tablespoon Worcestershire sauce

1 teaspoon sweet paprika

20 turns of freshly ground black pepper

Meatloaf is another one of those things that I didn't eat much as a kid. I learned to make it in culinary school and then perfected my technique by making it for staff meals in restaurants. There are a few things I've learned along the way. Anyone who has ever watched an episode of an Anthony Bourdain show has undoubtedly heard the old adage, fat is flavor. Which is true. Which is why you might be surprised to see that I call for very lean ground beef (90/10) in this recipe. When building a meatloaf, it's important to take into account how that flavor is imparted. If your meat is too fatty, the fat will render and the meatloaf will be greasy. Using a lean meat helps with the structure and the texture. The flavorful fat contribution comes from the bacon, eggs, and milk that deliver unctuousness while not compromising the structural integrity of the loaf. Cooking the garlic and onions with the bacon before they are mixed really makes a huge impact on the flavor and texture. Last, don't undermix the meat. The mixing helps create a tacky texture that helps the cohesiveness of the loaf when it bakes. This meatloaf is better on the second day.

1. **Make the meatloaf:** Preheat the oven to 375°F (190°C). Line a 9 × 5-inch (23 × 13cm) loaf pan with parchment paper.

RECIPE AND INGREDIENTS CONTINUE

FOR THE GLAZE:

6 tablespoons (105g) ketchup

2 tablespoons Dijon mustard

1 teaspoon blackstrap molasses

1 teaspoon apple cider vinegar

1 teaspoon Worcestershire sauce

½ teaspoon garlic powder

½ teaspoon onion powder

STORAGE: Allow to cool, then store in an airtight container in the refrigerator for up to 1 week. If freezing, allow the slices to cool before wrapping them individually and placing in the freezer.

2. Add the bacon to a large cold sauté pan. Set over medium heat and cook until the fat starts to render and color forms, about 5 minutes.

3. Add the onion and garlic and cook until they become soft and translucent, about 5 minutes. Remove from the heat and set aside to cool, about 10 minutes.

4. In a large bowl, mix the ground beef, ketchup, eggs, bread crumbs, parsley, milk, salt, Worcestershire sauce, sweet paprika, and pepper until well incorporated, about 5 minutes.

5. When the bacon/onion/garlic mixture has cooled down, add it to the ground beef mixture. Using your hands, mix the contents by squeezing large chunks together, making sure not to overmix. After a minute or so, the mixture will be slightly tacky and if you form a meatball, it will hold its shape.

6. Add the meatloaf mixture to the lined loaf pan, smoothing until it is of uniform height. It will be mounded in the pan. Tap the pan on the countertop to remove any air bubbles and to even out the meat.

7. Transfer to the oven and bake for 40 minutes.

8. Meanwhile, to make the glaze: In a small bowl, whisk together the ketchup, mustard, molasses, vinegar, Worcestershire sauce, garlic powder, and onion powder.

9. Remove the meatloaf from the oven and spread the glaze evenly atop the meatloaf in a thick coat with a silicone spatula. Return to the oven and bake until the internal temperature reaches 180° to 182°F (82° to 83°C), an additional 15 minutes.

10. Let sit for 15 minutes. Using a flat-edged spatula, slice the meatloaf into six 1½-inch (4cm) slices. Serve immediately.

SHEPHERD'S PIE

4 tablespoons (55g) unsalted butter

6 garlic cloves, roughly chopped

1 medium onion, finely diced

1½ pounds (680g) lean ground beef (90/10)

1½ pounds (680g) ground lamb

5 medium carrots, medium-diced

3 celery ribs, medium diced

¼ teaspoon ground ginger

½ teaspoon ground cumin

½ teaspoon smoked paprika

¼ teaspoon ground nutmeg

2 tablespoons (20g) kosher salt

1 cup (250ml) beef or chicken stock, store-bought or homemade (pages 38 and 36)

1 pound (168g) English peas, fresh or frozen but not canned

8 ounces (225g) sharp or medium cheddar cheese, shredded

Simple Fluffy Mashed Potatoes (page 205)

EQUIPMENT:

Rondeau

For hundreds of years, and probably much longer, shepherd's pie magically transformed leftovers into a filling and substantial meal. In earlier times, it was Scottish, Irish, and English families' way to give meat on its last legs a second life. By the time I first had it, while working as a cook at the now-closed Aqua restaurant in San Francisco, it was a way to turn all the trimmings and leftovers from service into a family meal. Back then, staff meal was generally terrible. Usually something made of potato peelings (from all the tourné potatoes we made) and tuna sinew or bloodline. But every few weeks, someone would realize we had enough meat trim to make a shepherd's pie. For me, as a young cook who couldn't afford to live in the city, who worked wild hours and relied on staff meal to eat, those days stick in my memory as bright ones. Later on, when I actually discovered the correct ratio of potatoes to meat (closer to 50/50 than the paltry 85/15 we had at Aqua), I grew to love the dish even more. When I serve it for Helena, it gives me the same comforted and taken-care-of feeling that was so rare when I was a young cook.

As with the lasagna (page 113), the fun (and most interactive part) of shepherd's pie is in the building of it.

1. Preheat the oven to 400°F (200°C). Place a sheet pan on the bottommost rack of the oven to catch drips.

RECIPE CONTINUES

2. Heat a rondeau over high heat. Once hot, add the butter and let it melt. Once the butter has melted and turned lightly browned, add the garlic and onion and cook until they begin to soften and take on some caramelization, about 5 minutes.

3. Add the ground meats to the onion and garlic, breaking them up with a wooden spoon or spatula. Once the meat starts to brown, after about 10 minutes, add the carrots and celery, stirring to combine. Add the ginger, cumin, smoked paprika, nutmeg, and salt, stirring to combine.

4. Stir in the stock, making sure to scrape up any stuck bits from the sides and bottom of the rondeau with a wooden spoon. Once the carrots and celery are tender and the liquid is reduced, about 5 minutes, add the peas and cook for 30 seconds. Remove the pan from the heat and transfer the contents to a 9 × 13-inch (23 × 33cm) baking dish, smoothing it evenly with a spatula. Set aside.

5. Fold the shredded cheddar into the mashed potatoes and then scoop them over the meat and vegetables, spreading the potatoes evenly in a thick layer.

6. Bake until the top is golden and crispy in spots, about 45 minutes.

7. Let rest for 10 minutes before serving.

SALADS

IF I COULD SELL YOU A BOOK THAT COULD GET KIDS excited to eat salads, I'd be a very rich man. If you could write a book doing the same, I'd buy it and you'd be a rich man. Sadly, I haven't cracked the code to get Helena and Niko to adore salads all the time. But I have come across a few incremental commonsense steps that make it slightly more likely that salad ends up in their mouths and not pushed into a pile on their plates.

You can't blame a kid for not loving a salad made of watery tasteless out-of-season vegetables. Salads are, by design, made to showcase the freshness of the product. Make sure that the salad isn't boring: Vary the textures. Add some crunch. Maybe something creamy. Something citrusy.

Also introduce your kids to vegetables when they—the vegetables, not the kids—are at the peak of their flavor.

That being said, there's a reason I don't have fifteen salads in the book. I've limited myself to those that are fun and approachable. But if you want to explore, do it. The dressings—Caesar Dressing (page 184) and Red Wine Vinaigrette (page 189)—work on a ton of different salad and lettuce configurations. And if you want more salad recipes, wait until my next book, *Cooking for Your Own Damn Self*!

WEEKNIGHT
MEAL

TOMATO AND BREAD SALAD

½ loaf (11 ounces/300g) country levain, sourdough, or any other crusty bread

½ cup (120ml) extra-virgin olive oil

½ cup (135g) Dijon mustard

1½ teaspoons (5g) kosher salt

40 turns freshly ground black pepper

1 pound 11 ounces (760g) large heirloom tomatoes (3 to 4), cut into 1- to 2-inch (2.5 to 5cm) chunks

½ medium red onion, thinly sliced on the grain (from root to stem)

1 large yellow bell pepper, cut into 1- to 2-inch (2.5 to 5cm) chunks

2 to 3 Persian (mini) cucumbers, cut into ½-inch (13mm) coins

1 tablespoon (16g) coarse sea salt

¼ cup red or white wine vinegar

1 garlic clove, grated on a Microplane or finely chopped

Panzanella, the Tuscan bread salad (see page 180 for photo) that this kinda is, is one of those last-chance food user-uppers. (Fattoush, which this also resembles, is the same but from the Levant.) In those cases, it's the bread that needed eating. Here, however, the salad serves a different but equally practical purpose. Helena—like most kids— will eat bread for days but salad only barely. Tomato and bread salad is a ninja hack. It's the flavors—and sustenance—of salad but camouflaged with chunks of stale (or crusty) bread. This has more vegetables than the traditional panzanella, which add some texture and crunch, and, because it's me making it, an almost excessive amount of herbs. If the empty bowls are an indication, its vegetable-delivery subterfuge is a success.

1. Preheat the oven to 375°F (190°C). Line a sheet pan with parchment paper.

2. Cut the bread loaf in half, horizontally, as if making a sandwich, then slice lengthwise into strips. Cut the strips crosswise into chunks, roughly 1 × 2 inches (2.5 × 5cm). Place the bread in a large bowl. Add the olive oil, mustard, kosher salt, and pepper. Toss the bread to coat. Spread the coated bread onto the sheet pan in one layer.

3. Bake for 20 minutes. Remove, stir around, and bake until dark golden brown and crispy, another 5 minutes. Remove from the oven and set aside.

FOR THE DRESSING:

1 tablespoon whole-grain mustard or Dijon mustard

Grated zest and juice of 1 large lemon (Meyer if available)

⅓ cup (80ml) extra-virgin olive oil

2 large pinches of coarse sea salt

Generous amount freshly ground black pepper

ASSEMBLY:

½ bunch fresh basil (¾ ounce/ 20g), leaves picked and torn

¼ bunch fresh mint (½ ounce/ 10g), leaves picked and torn

½ bunch Italian parsley (1 ounce/30g), chopped, including stems

4. In a large bowl, combine the tomatoes, onion, bell pepper, and cucumbers. Sprinkle the coarse sea salt over the vegetables and toss. Add in the vinegar and garlic. Marinate for a minimum of 5 minutes.

5. **Make the dressing:** In a small bowl, whisk together the mustard, lemon zest, lemon juice, olive oil, sea salt, and black pepper until it comes together.

6. **Assemble the salad:** Place the toasted bread chunks in a large bowl with the marinated vegetables. Toss together for 10 to 15 seconds so the bread starts to absorb some of the juice and vinegar. Add the herbs. Pour the dressing over the vegetables. Gently toss the salad together for 30 to 40 seconds, to coat all the ingredients. Serve immediately.

No Tomatoes?

A tomato and bread salad relies on really good tomatoes. Such tomatoes aren't always available. Rather than use crap tomatoes, substitute with roasted squash.

1 large winter squash, seeded, peeled, if needed, and cut into 1- to 2-inch (2.5 to 5cm) chunks (about 1½ pounds/ 680g)

2 tablespoons (25g) olive oil

Kosher salt and freshly ground black pepper

Preheat the oven to 400°F (200°C). Place the squash on a sheet pan. Add the olive oil and season with salt and pepper. Toss to coat. Roast until fork-tender, 45 minutes to 1 hour.

CAESAR SALAD

3 romaine hearts, bottoms removed but leaves whole

½ recipe Judy Rodgers's Croutons (page 187)

½ cup (120ml) Caesar Dressing (recipe follows)

Generous amount grated Parmigiano-Reggiano cheese, for serving

Freshly ground black pepper, for serving

EQUIPMENT:

Salad spinner

It's inherited wisdom that kids don't like anchovies. True, Helena might not be a fan of entire little fishies, but I can tell you she loves the umami they bring to this dressing. As far as the salad goes, you do you. I love the crispness of the classic romaine, but it also works well with chicories, which are slightly more bitter.

A salad spinner, which you'll need here for the romaine hearts, is the most fun of the semi-useless kitchen equipment . . . and a lesson in centrifugal force.

1. Add half of the romaine and half of the croutons to a large salad bowl. Pour half of the dressing over. Add the rest of the romaine and croutons. Pour the remaining dressing over them. Toss gently until everything is well coated.

2. Add a generous amount of parmesan and black pepper on top to serve.

CAESAR DRESSING

Extra dressing can be used as a condiment for Save Your Ass Grilled Chicken (page 137) or Chicken (or Anything) Milanese (page 142).

MAKES 1½ CUPS (360ML)

2 fresh egg yolks

4 garlic cloves, peeled but whole

4 oil-packed anchovy fillets

RECIPE AND INGREDIENTS CONTINUE

2 tablespoons Dijon mustard

1 teaspoon Worcestershire sauce

Juice of 2 lemons

1 tablespoon red wine vinegar

2 teaspoons (8g) kosher salt

1 cup (250ml) extra-virgin olive oil

1 teaspoon freshly ground black pepper

In a food processor, combine the egg yolks, garlic, anchovies, mustard, Worcestershire sauce, lemon juice, vinegar, and salt and blend until smooth. With the food processor running, slowly drizzle in the olive oil until emulsified. Add the pepper at the end and blend until combined.

JUDY RODGERS'S CROUTONS

1 loaf country bread, cut into 1-inch (2.5cm) cubes

2 large garlic cloves, grated

½ cup (135g) Dijon mustard

1½ tablespoons (12g) kosher salt

½ teaspoon freshly ground black pepper

Grated zest of ½ lemon

4 tablespoons extra-virgin olive oil

These are an adaptation of Judy Rodgers's croutons from Zuni Café. I say adaptation because I saw the recipe once, made it, and loved it. Judy is someone I draw a lot of inspiration from; nevertheless, I'm not going to cook from anyone else's recipe. Rather, I use it as a starting point. I encourage you to do the same thing. Adjust as you go. The bread will vary tremendously. I prefer a country bread which isn't as sour as a levain or a sourdough. The mustard helps elevate these croutons from just crunchy bits of bread to an immensely snackable lure in any salad. Use these croutons in all the salads (especially the Tomato and Bread Salad, page 182) plus Stracciatella (page 55) and Buttery Tomato Soup (page 52).

1. Preheat the oven to 425°F (220°C) (or 400°F/200°C for convection). Line two half-sheet pans with parchment paper.

2. In a large bowl, toss together the bread cubes, garlic, mustard, salt, pepper, lemon zest, and olive oil. Spread them evenly on the sheet pans.

3. Bake for 10 minutes and stir. Bake until golden and crispy, another 10 minutes.

STORAGE: Allow to cool, then store in an airtight container in the refrigerator for up to 3 days. When ready to use, refresh at 375°F (190°C) for 5 minutes.

CHOPPED SALAD WITH RED WINE VINAIGRETTE

12 ounces (340g) chopped salad lettuces, such as Little Gems, romaine, or butter lettuce

Kosher salt and freshly ground black pepper

½ cup (120ml) Red Wine Vinaigrette (recipe follows)

1 tablespoon red wine vinegar

3 spring onions (50g), thinly sliced into rings, or an equivalent amount of the white parts of leeks

½ cup (80g) packed pitted Castelvetrano olives, halved

⅔ cup (130g) canned chickpeas, drained and rinsed

¾ cup (3½ ounces/100g) diced salami

¾ cup (3½ ounces/100g) diced provolone cheese

¾ cup (3½ ounces/100g) sliced pepperoncini

¼ cup (5g) finely chopped fresh dill

2 tablespoons freshly grated Parmigiano-Reggiano cheese

Whether you call this a salad or a sandwich without the bread depends on how virtuous you are trying to appear. I belong to the school of self-love, so yes, a chopped salad is a salad and this chopped salad is Helena's favorite. The salami and the cheese make it an easy introduction to the genre. Even if she's not scarfing the lettuce, she is, technically, still eating a salad. That's a win.

If your kid has level II skills—chopping—there's plenty to help with in this salad. Much of the ingredients here are harder, dense, and uniform, which makes chopping easier (and safer).

1. Place the lettuces in a large salad bowl. Season with salt and pepper. Pour the vinaigrette and the red wine vinegar around the sides of the bowl.

2. Add the spring onions, olives, chickpeas, salami, provolone, pepperoncini, and dill. Toss gently with your hands to evenly coat and season each element.

3. Top with the grated parmesan. Serve immediately.

RED WINE VINAIGRETTE

Red wine vinaigrette is a good go-to dressing for all types of salad, plus it keeps virtually forever in the fridge. It also makes a great marinade for chicken breast.

MAKES 2 CUPS (470ML)

½ cup (120ml) red wine vinegar

2 garlic cloves, grated on a Microplane

1½ tablespoons (15g) kosher salt

Juice of ½ lemon (1 teaspoon/10g)

1 tablespoon Dijon mustard

1¾ cups (420ml) extra-virgin olive oil

1 tablespoon chile flakes

1½ tablespoons dried oregano

1. In a small bowl, whisk together the vinegar, garlic, salt, lemon juice, and mustard. Allow to marinate for 15 minutes.

2. In a small saucepan, combine ½ cup (120ml) of the olive oil, the chile flakes, and oregano. Gently heat over medium-high heat until the oil is fragrant.

3. Remove from the heat and add the remaining 1¼ cups (300ml) oil to cool down the warmed oil.

4. While whisking vigorously, emulsify the oil into the vinegar mixture until a creamy texture is achieved. Place in a small bowl and cool to room temperature.

VEGGIES

MANY PARENTS OUT THERE HAVE RESIGNED THEMSELVES to the fact that their kids just don't eat vegetables. I get it. It's hard to fight the fight all the time. If you feed your kids vegetables often when they are really young, then I think it's easier to develop that habit. But that doesn't change the fact that kids and vegetables don't always get along.

My daughter, Helena, goes through phases with veggies. She will decide that she doesn't like carrots this week or doesn't like zucchini the next. I've found that adding lemon or bathing them in tomato sauce helps and, if that fails, I can usually bribe her with dessert. What I do know is that texture plays a big role in getting your kids liking veggies. If they are super overcooked and mushy, your kids won't like them just like you wouldn't. So, the recipes in this chapter focus on getting the best, most kid-friendly textures possible. The same goes with grains.

Because most of these are meant to be side dishes, I've also gone ahead and selected a few recipes that I think go well that you can pair to make a full meal. But really most of these veggies go with most everything else.

TANGY COLLARD GREENS WITH LEMON AND CHILE FLAKES

½ cup (120ml) extra-virgin olive oil

1 medium yellow onion, thinly sliced

1 pound 5 ounces (600g) collard greens, washed, stemmed, and chiffonaded

1½ tablespoons (15g) kosher salt

Thinly sliced peel and juice of 2 medium lemons

Pinch of chile flakes

This classic Brazilian preparation, in which the greens are chiffonaded (cut into narrow strips) and then quickly steamed, turned me into a real collard greens believer. With the addition of the heat and acid from the chile flake and lemon, respectively, these collards stand on their own.

A note about the size of collard greens: A bunch of collards can be the size of a softball or the size of your head. So instead of giving you a number of bunches, I've given a weight instead.

Dark and leafy, collard greens are one of the best sources of folate, a vitamin that is especially important for children.

STORAGE: Allow to cool, then store in an airtight container in the refrigerator for up to 3 days.

GOES WELL WITH:

"Jew-ish" Fried Chicken (page 152) • Weeknight Meal

Simple Fluffy Mashed Potatoes (page 205) • Weeknight Meal

Fennel and Calabrian Chili-Roasted Pork Rib Rack (page 157) • Weeknight Meal

1. In a heavy-bottomed pot, heat the olive oil over high heat. Add the onion and sweat it, making sure it does not develop any color, about 2 minutes. Add the collard greens directly over the onion, using tongs to stir in the onions (and off of the bottom of the pot).

2. Add the salt and lemon peel and stir well. Cover the pot and reduce the heat to medium, allowing the greens to steam for 3 to 4 minutes.

3. Uncover, letting the condensation that has gathered drop back into the pot. Stir the collards and cook for another minute or so. Add the lemon juice and chile flakes (if using), stir again, and let cook for 3 minutes. Turn off the heat, and allow to rest for 5 minutes before enjoying.

LEMONY BUTTER
BEANS,
page 202

CREAMY SHAVED
BRUSSELS SPROUTS
WITH BACON,
page 204

CREAMY CORN AND
GREEN BEANS,
page 198

CRISPY ROASTED
SWEET-AND-SOUR
MUSHROOMS,
page 211

CREAMY CORN AND GREEN BEANS

1 tablespoon (15g) unsalted butter

½ medium yellow onion, finely diced

4 ears corn, shucked, and kernels cut off the cob

1 pound (450g) green beans, trimmed and cut into ¼-inch (6mm) pieces

Thinly sliced peel and juice of 1 medium lemon

1 tablespoon (10g) kosher salt

1 cup (250ml) heavy cream

¼ teaspoon freshly ground black pepper

Pinch of chile flakes (optional)

EQUIPMENT:

Rondeau

GOES WELL WITH:

Miso Honey Mustard Baked Chicken (page 140) • Weeknight Meal

''Jew-ish'' Fried Chicken (page 152) • Weeknight Meal

The Best Fricking Meatloaf in the World (page 173) • Project Cooking

Corn is an easy sell for kids. It's sweet. It's fun to eat. You get to shuck it. Green beans are less of an easy sell. They're green. They're beans. They taste . . . healthy. But this comforting recipe is a good way to marry the two. (The cream adds richness; the lemon keeps it from being too much.) It's the perfect quick side dish for steak night or a BBQ or fried chicken or meatloaf. Plus, who doesn't like to shuck?

Shucking Party! The fastest shucker gets a prize. (That prize can be choosing what to watch during family screen time.)

1. Heat a rondeau over high heat, then add the butter and let melt. Once the foaming has subsided, add the onion, stirring constantly so it doesn't brown. After a minute, add the corn kernels, stirring frequently for 2 minutes. Add the green beans, stirring for another minute. Add the lemon peel and salt, stirring for 2 minutes.

To make this lighter, omit the cream entirely and replace the butter with extra-virgin olive oil.

2. Add the cream, pepper, and chile flakes (if using). Allow the cream to cook down and thicken, until it coats the back of the spoon (nappé, if you're being technical), about 3 minutes. Remove from the heat and stir in the lemon juice.

3. Set back over high heat and cook for another minute or so until the cream has cooked down enough that it is nappé.

Remove from the heat but continue stirring for a minute or two. As the sauce cools it will thicken further and emulsify. Serve immediately.

ROMANO BEANS, PEPPERS, ONIONS, AND STEWED TOMATOES (SPICY OR NOT)

MELTDOWN MEAL

⅓ cup (80ml) extra-virgin olive oil

1 medium yellow onion, thinly sliced

1 large red bell pepper, cut into thin strips

1 pound (450g) Romano beans

One 14.5-ounce (411g) can crushed tomatoes

Pinch of chili flakes (optional)

1 tablespoon (10g) kosher salt

Thinly sliced peel and juice of 1 large lemon

EQUIPMENT:

Rondeau

GOES WELL WITH:

Save Your Ass Grilled Chicken (page 137) • Meltdown Meal

Shrimp fra Diavolo (page 131) • Meltdown Meal

Smothered Italian Sausage (page 139) • Meltdown Meal

This is an odds-and-ends dish, so think of the ingredients listed as suggestions. Feel free to improvise based on what you have. You can use any type of bean you want—French green beans, Chinese long beans, yellow long beans. I just had some Romanos from my garden about to go bad. There's no trick here, just technique. You want to pull as much of the water out of the tomato sauce as possible so it sticks to the beans, rather than have the beans swimming in it. When I make this for my family, I use only a couple of chile flakes, but I personally like it on the spicier side.

Depending how spice tolerant your kids are, add a lot, a little, or no chile flakes.

1. In a rondeau, heat the olive oil over high heat until it shimmers. Add the onion, stirring constantly until translucent, about 3 minutes. Stir in the bell peppers and cook for about 2 minutes. Add the beans and cook for 3 minutes.

2. Add the tomatoes and chile flakes (if using) and cook until the sauce begins to thicken, about 5 minutes. Season with the salt, lemon peel, and juice. Stir for an additional 3 minutes and then serve.

STORAGE: Allow to cool, then store in an airtight container in the refrigerator for up to 5 days.

LEMONY BUTTER BEANS

⅔ cup (160ml) extra-virgin olive oil

8 medium garlic cloves, roughly chopped

1 medium yellow onion, finely diced

2 tender celery stalks, finely diced

Finely sliced peel and juice of 1 large lemon

Two 15-ounce (425g) cans butter beans, undrained

1 tablespoon (10g) kosher salt

1 ounce (28g) fresh Italian parsley, roughly chopped

EQUIPMENT:

Rondeau

NOTE: *I use butter beans but you can use other large white beans like Great Northern or Corona.*

Here's a secret: Sometimes when we chefs write menus, we just come up with a bunch of ingredients that we think will go well together. Sometimes the recipes work; sometimes they don't. I made these lemony butter beans for a private party at Che Fico. I had never made them before, but, even after caviar and truffles, these beans were all the guests talked about. At home, they're nearly as big a hit, where these seemingly unassuming beans surprise with big bold flavors. Butter beans hold up to being boiled, retaining their shape but still being creamy inside, while the onion provides enough texture to avoid monotony and the lemon a zing of flavor.

Butter beans, also called lima beans, are high in protein and fiber and help maintain strong and healthy bones.

Use these beans to replace potatoes or another starch, when accompanying a veggie and a protein.

1. In a rondeau, heat the olive oil over high heat until it shimmers, but not smoking. Add the garlic, onion, and celery and cook, stirring constantly, until they become fragrant, about 1 minute. Add the lemon peel and allow to cook for three minutes.

2. Add the butter beans and their liquid, stirring constantly, until the liquid reduces and emulsifies with the olive oil, about 3 minutes. Add the lemon juice and salt, stirring

GOES WELL WITH:

Smothered Italian Sausage
(page 139) • Meltdown Meal

Fennel and Calabrian Chili-
Roasted Pork Rib Rack
(page 157) • Weeknight Meal

occasionally. Cook until the consistency begins to look creamy, about 5 minutes.

3. Turn off the heat and add the parsley. Serve immediately.

STORAGE: Allow to cool, then store in an airtight container in the refrigerator for up to 5 days.

CREAMY SHAVED BRUSSELS SPROUTS WITH BACON

1½ tablespoons extra-virgin olive oil

5¼ ounces (150g) smoked bacon (4 to 5 slices), cut into matchstick-sized pieces

½ medium Spanish onion, sliced on the grain (from root to stem)

1 pound (454g) Brussels sprouts, shaved on a mandoline

1 tablespoon Dijon mustard

⅓ cup (80ml) heavy cream

Thinly sliced peel of 2 large lemons

½ cup (120ml) fresh lemon juice

Kosher salt (optional)

GOES WELL WITH:

Save Your Ass Grilled Chicken (page 137) • Meltdown Meal

''Jew-ish'' Fried Chicken (page 152) • Weeknight Meal

The Best Fricking Meatloaf in the World (page 173) • Project Cooking

Brussel sprouts might not be the first thing you reach for when you want a low stress dinner without a fight, but I've found that with the correct preparation the whole family will love them. There are a few ways to go about coaxing the right flavor and texture out of these mini cabbage heads. One is to cut them in half and fry them in olive oil until they are crispy, then drench them in lemon juice. Another is to shave them super thin and melt them down with devious fats like bacon and cream.

If you want a more low-cal version, shave the Brussels sprouts thin and toss them with vinaigrette, olive oil, dried fruits, and nuts.

In a Dutch oven, heat the oil over high heat. Add the bacon to the pot and cook to render the fat, 1 to 2 minutes. Add the onion and cook for 1 to 2 minutes, stirring occasionally. Add the Brussels sprouts and stir until they begin to caramelize, about 3 minutes. Stir in the mustard, then add the heavy cream and stir to coat the vegetables in the cream. Cook for about 2 minutes, then remove from the heat. Stir in the lemon peel and juice. Taste and season with salt if desired. Serve immediately.

STORAGE: Allow to cool, then store in an airtight container in the refrigerator for up to 5 days

SIMPLE FLUFFY MASHED POTATOES

4 large russet potatoes (about 12 ounces/340g each), scrubbed, peeled, and halved crosswise

Kosher salt

3 sticks (12 ounces/340g) unsalted butter

1⅔ cups (400ml) whole milk

Ground white pepper

STORAGE: Allow to cool, then store in an airtight container in the refrigerator for up to 1 week.

GOES WELL WITH:

The question is what do mashed potatoes *not* go well with?

A fluffy mashed potato recipe should be in every dad's repertoire. Over the years, like many cooks, I've been lured down the path of overcomplication. I've added roasted garlic, fresh herbs, sour cream, parmesan, even ranch dressing, to my mashed potatoes. Those were good, but this is great. Thanks to the starchiness of the russet potato, you end up with something super fluffy, airy, and buttery. It immediately transports me to my childhood—KFC and boxed mashed potatoes—back when eating meaningless carbs wasn't even a thought.

1. In a large soup pot, combine the potatoes with cold water to cover. Salt the water generously. Bring the potatoes to a light simmer over medium heat and cook until tender, about 40 minutes.

2. When the potatoes are almost done, in a small saucepan, melt the butter and milk over medium heat.

3. Once the potatoes are fully cooked, drain them in a colander and immediately return them to the pot with the heat turned off. Cover and allow them to steam for 2 minutes in their residual liquid.

4. Uncover and add half the milk/butter mixture, mashing the potatoes with a masher or a fork until mostly broken up. Add the rest of the milk/butter mixture, mashing until the potatoes have a creamy consistency. Season with salt and white pepper and serve immediately.

MY SO-CALLED CURRY

2 cups (370g) jasmine rice

FOR THE "CURRY"

⅓ cup (80ml) extra-virgin olive oil

7 large garlic cloves, roughly chopped

2-inch (5cm) knob fresh ginger (½ ounce/15g), peeled and finely diced

2 tablespoons tomato paste

1 large globe eggplant (1 pound/450g), diced

2 tablespoons (18g) kosher salt, plus more to taste

5 carrots, peeled and cut into ½-inch (13mm) coins

1 yellow onion, diced

1 red bell pepper, diced

3 (13.5-ounce/400ml) cans unsweetened coconut milk

1 stalk lemongrass

1 (14.5-ounce/411g) can diced tomatoes, undrained

2 (15-ounce/425g) cans chickpeas, rinsed and drained

Juice of 2 limes (60g)

1 pound 5 ounces (600g) zucchini (about 4), diced

As I said before, cooking for family meal in professional kitchens is great training for cooking at home for your actual family. Time is always tight; money often is, too. It's an important part of your day but not actually your job. But you can tell a lot by how and what kind of meal a chef provides. This curry grew out of my days cooking family meal. I used to keep a case of #10 cans of coconut milk—that's over 12 cups (3L) each— on hand just for this. It's full of affordable but nutritious vegetables: horse carrots (those are those big carrots you see), globe eggplants, celery. The chickpeas offer not just flavor and texture but a kick of protein, too.

1. Rinse the rice in cold water until the water runs clear. Drain and place the rice in the bowl of a rice cooker. Add enough water so that it comes above the rice by one knuckle (touch the top of the rice with a finger and the water should come to the first knuckle). Follow the rice cooker instructions to cook the rice.

2. Meanwhile, make the "curry": In a large heavy-bottomed pot or rondeau, heat the olive oil over high heat. Add the garlic and ginger and cook until they are fragrant and lightly browned, about 1 minute. Add the tomato paste, breaking it up, and fry with the garlic and ginger for about 1 minute.

3. Stir in the eggplant, which will absorb most of the olive oil in the pot. Add the salt to the eggplant. This will help it

1¼ pounds (575g) baby bok choy (about 5), quartered lengthwise and cut into 1-inch (2.5cm) pieces

1 bunch cilantro (3½ ounces/90g), leaves and stems, roughly chopped

Freshly ground black pepper

2 tablespoons honey

EQUIPMENT:

Rice cooker

STORAGE: As with most stews and soups, this recipe only gets better with time. It will last in the fridge for up to 1 week, but I would not recommend freezing it.

release moisture and you will hear it start to sizzle. There will be some color forming at the bottom of the pan; this is okay, as long as it doesn't turn black. Cook the eggplant until softened, 3 to 4 minutes.

4. Add the carrots and onion, stirring together, for about 2 minutes. Add the bell pepper and cook for about 1 minute.

5. Add the coconut milk. Break up the lemongrass stalk by bending it and add to the pot. Cook for about 1 minute. Add the diced tomatoes and their juice and continue to cook over high heat, stirring occasionally, for 4 to 5 minutes. Add the chickpeas and cook until the carrots are slightly tender, 10 to 12 minutes.

6. Add the lime juice, zucchini, bok choy, and cilantro. Stir to combine and cook for 3 to 4 minutes.

7. Add black pepper to taste. Stir in the honey and continue to cook for about 5 minutes, stirring occasionally. Add more salt to taste. When ready the sauce should coat the back of a spoon.

8. Serve immediately in a bowl, spooned over rice.

NOTE: *You can remove the lemongrass stalk or keep it in. Just don't eat it.*

GARLIC OLIVE OIL FRIED EGGPLANT, FRESH MOZZARELLA, AND TOMATOES

MELTDOWN MEAL

1 pound 6 ounces eggplant (about 2), preferably Japanese or Chinese, cut on the bias into slices 1½ inches (4cm) thick

1⅓ cups (320ml) plus 2 tablespoons extra-virgin olive oil

Kosher salt

6 garlic cloves, smashed

14 ounces (400g) cherry tomatoes (about 1⅓ cups)

½ cup (12g) packed fresh basil leaves, plus 8 or 9 leaves for garnish

1 tablespoon balsamic vinegar, preferably aged

1 (8-ounce/225g) ball fresh mozzarella, cut into slices ½ inch (13mm) thick

Pinch of flaky sea salt

Eggplant can have the most wonderful creamy texture—or be unappealingly chewy and sponge-like. There is no better way to ensure the former than to fry it in olive oil, which yields an almost custardy silky consistency. Plus, eggplant is great at soaking up the flavors of its compatriots, in this case tomatoes and mozzarella. This is basically pasta alla Norma without the pasta.

1. Preheat the oven to 375°F (190°C).

2. In a bowl, toss the eggplant with ⅓ cup (80ml) of the olive oil and 1½ teaspoons (5g) kosher salt.

3. In a large skillet, heat 1 cup (240ml) of the olive oil over high heat until it shimmers. Working in batches to avoid crowding the pan, carefully lay the eggplant in the oil in one layer. The eggplant should sizzle but the oil should not smoke. Fry until golden brown, about 3 minutes. Flip and brown on the other side for another 3 minutes.

4. Place the browned eggplant in a 9 × 13-inch (23 × 33cm) baking dish. Repeat with the rest of the eggplant pieces.

5. After all the eggplant has been cooked, add the smashed garlic to the hot oil and cook until golden brown. Add the tomatoes, a pinch of salt, and the basil immediately after. At this point, the oil might spit, so if you have a lid, put it on top

RECIPE CONTINUES

GOES WELL WITH:

Chopped Salad with Red Wine Vinaigrette (page 188) • Meltdown Meal

Spaghetti and Meatballs (page 149) • Meltdown Meal

of the pan. The oil will still pop and spit, so be careful. Sauté for 2 minutes.

6. Pour the garlic and tomatoes over the eggplant and spread evenly. (The dish can be assembled to this point and refrigerated. When you're ready to cook, bring it to room temperature for 30 minutes.)

7. Bake for 10 minutes.

8. Remove from the oven, and drizzle the balsamic vinegar over the top. Place the mozzarella slices on top.

9. Return to the oven until the mozzarella is melted, another 5 to 6 minutes.

10. To serve, finish with the remaining 2 tablespoons olive oil, the basil leaves, and the flaky salt.

Day Two

If you have a lot of leftovers and want to repurpose them as pasta, boil a short noodle like rigatoni or fusilli in salted water, drain (reserving about 1 cup of pasta water), and return to the pot. Add the leftovers directly to the hot pasta and toss together in the warm pot, adding pasta water as needed to rewarm. Reseason with some parmesan and chile flakes, if so desired.

CRISPY ROASTED SWEET-AND-SOUR MUSHROOMS

WEEKNIGHT
MEAL

1 pound (450g) hen of the woods (maitake) mushrooms, in large clusters

¼ cup (60ml) plus 1 tablespoon extra-virgin olive oil

1½ teaspoons (5g) kosher salt

Freshly ground black pepper

2 tablespoons (30g) unsalted butter

1 medium onion, thinly sliced along the grain (from root to stem)

4 tablespoons red wine vinegar

Hen of the woods mushrooms look crazy. Where they grow in the forest, they resemble a bird nestling at the base of a tree. Once at home, they look like some kind of alien brain. Kids love it. Kids also love texture, which—as a chef—is also what draws me to hen of the woods (also called maitake) mushrooms. Because they're not as waterlogged as a porcini or button mushroom, they get super crispy. I could eat crispy well-salted hen of the woods on their own—the combination of crunch and earthiness is irresistible.

Adding sweetness, thanks to the sweet-and-sour onion, and crunch helps even picky eaters explore new foods.

1. Preheat the oven to 450°F (convection if available). Line a sheet pan with aluminum foil.

2. Evenly spread the mushrooms on the pan, drizzle with ¼ cup (60ml) of the olive oil, and season with salt and pepper to taste.

3. Roast until golden brown and crispy, 25 to 30 minutes.

4. Meanwhile, heat a medium sauté pan over medium-high heat. Add the butter and once melted and slightly browned, add the onion. Stir to coat the onion with butter. Add the remaining ½ teaspoon salt and cook for about 3 minutes. Once the onion starts to lightly caramelize, add

RECIPE CONTINUES

GOES WELL WITH:

One-Dish Halibut with
Summer Vegetables
(page 128) • Weeknight Meal

Crispy Skin Pan-Roasted
Salmon with Tomato Basil
Relish (page 160) •
Weeknight Meal

Shepherd's Pie (page 175) •
Project Cooking

3 tablespoons of the red wine vinegar. Allow the liquid to cook down until it starts to look glaze-y and to coat the onion. Remove from the heat.

5. Remove the mushrooms from the oven and place in a large bowl. Top with the sweet-and-sour onion with a large spoon, encouraging them to fall into the cracks of the mushrooms. Drizzle with the remaining 1 tablespoon red wine vinegar and 1 tablespoon olive oil. Serve immediately.

ZUCCHINI PARMIGIANA

3 medium zucchini (about
7 ounces/200g each), cut into
1½-inch (4cm) coins

2 cups (470ml) Pomodoro Sauce
(page 47; see Note)

Kosher salt

⅔ cup freshly grated Parmigiano-
Reggiano cheese (2 ounces/55g)

1½ tablespoons extra-virgin
olive oil

4 or 5 fresh basil leaves,
for garnish

No one family can eat all the zucchini coming its way during the summer—my garden practically spews out fully formed zucchini like an assembly line—but you can, and you probably should, try to use as much as you can. Zucchini is packed with vitamins and antioxidants, including vitamin A, which boosts the immune system. The problem? It's not necessarily packed with flavor. The good news is that means it's versatile. You can make zucchini bread, zucchini fritters, zucchini noodles. In this simple side dish, the zucchini is mostly a vehicle for tomato sauce and parmesan. Besides nutrients, it adds texture, so it's important not to let it get mushy, which is why I cut the zucchini slices relatively thick.

Kids can help cut the zucchini into coins. Don't worry about whether they're uniform. (Or if you care that much, discreetly adjust them later.)

Don't use a gigantic zucchini. It'll be too watery.

1. Preheat the oven to 450°F.

2. Place the zucchini coins in a 9 × 13-inch (23 × 33cm) baking dish.

3. Taste the pomodoro sauce and add salt to taste. Pour the sauce over the zucchini, making sure it covers it, and top with the parmesan cheese. Drizzle with the olive oil.

GOES WELL WITH:

Chopped Salad with Red Wine Vinaigrette (page 188) • Meltdown Meal

Garlic Bread (page 237) • Weeknight Meal

Any of the pastas on pages 79 through 118

4. Bake until the zucchini is tender but not mushy, 30 to 40 minutes (depending on the water content of your pomodoro sauce and zucchini).

5. Serve garnished with basil leaves.

NOTE: *If you don't have homemade pomodoro on hand, a jar of good store-bought pomodoro sauce will work. Keep in mind that store-bought sauce tends to be more watery than my version and the last thing you want is a soup-y parmigiana. So, before you start, heat the sauce over medium heat in a small saucepan for 10 minutes until it is slightly reduced. Make sure you check the seasoning.*

ZUCCHINI
PARMIGIANA,
page 214

WEEKNIGHT
MEAL

GLAZED CARROTS
WITH LIME JUICE AND BUTTER

2 tablespoons (30g) unsalted butter

2 bunches carrots (1½ pounds/ 650g total), tops removed, peeled and cut into 1-inch (2.5cm) pieces

½ medium yellow onion, thinly sliced

2 cups (450ml) beef stock (page 38)

1 teaspoon (3g) kosher salt

Juice of 1 large or 2 small limes

Glazed carrots are hardly earth-shattering. The dinner plates of America are filled with these bright and shiny batons that hover just on the savory side of the dessert divide. What I like about this version—which I make often— is that by substituting beef stock for the honey and lime juice for the more common orange juice, the carrots get an additional nutritional element with a ton of flavor while not sacrificing the pleasing glaze. The sweetness comes from the onion. The result is a punchy side dish that's both familiar enough to soothe and novel enough to intrigue.

Have your little sous peel and cut up the carrots.

Making a glaze out of beef stock, rather than honey, gives the carrots an additional nutritional kick (without the sugar).

1. Add the butter to a cold Dutch oven or deep heavy-bottomed pan. Heat over high heat until the butter melts. Once the butter has melted, add the carrots, stirring to coat. Allow the carrots to caramelize, about 6 minutes, stirring every 2 to 3 minutes.

2. Stir in the onion, reduce the heat to medium to avoid burning the onion, and cook for about 3 minutes. Add the beef stock, increase the heat to high, and bring to a rapid simmer or a low boil, about 4 minutes. Once simmering, add the salt and lime juice and continue to allow the stock to reduce, about 5 minutes.

3. Once the liquid has dropped below the carrots, stir to prevent the sauce from scorching. Cook for another 5 minutes, until you can draw a line in the glaze at the bottom of the pot with the back of a spoon.

4. Remove the pot from the heat and continue stirring until the carrots are well coated. If the glaze doesn't adhere to the carrots, return to the heat for a few minutes more to further reduce. Serve immediately.

CREAMY POLENTA

6 cups (1.4L) whole milk
(see Note)

1¾ cups (8½ ounces/240g)
polenta

Kosher salt

8 ounces (225g) Parmigiano-
Reggiano cheese, grated

People rarely cook polenta at home in the United States, but it's the workhorse starch in the north of Italy, especially around Piedmont, Veneto, and Friuli. I'm a big proponent. It has all the creaminess of grits, which is why my kids love it, and it can soak up all the sauces and juices from things like sausage and peppers or Calabrian pork rack. As a parent, I love it because it's easy to make a large batch, cool it, freeze it, and reheat when you need. As a whole, polenta varies widely because, well, we're talking about corn. Some is deep red. Some is bright green. Some is taupe or beige or white. Some take longer to cook than others. Some is coarse and others are fine. Use this recipe as a guideline, but be flexible. When finished, the polenta should be creamy without much bite.

Successful polenta requires constant stirring so it doesn't clump. Let your kid do it.

1. In a large heavy-bottomed pot that is at least 8 quarts (7.5L), bring the milk to a simmer over high heat, about 5 minutes. If a slight skin forms on the surface, it should be ready.

2. Gradually add the polenta to the milk, whisking it in as you go. Don't add it all at once or it will stick to the bottom. Once incorporated, drop the heat to low. Add a pinch of salt. Stir constantly to make sure nothing sticks to the bottom of

STORAGE: Polenta will last a week and a half in the fridge and up to 3 months in the freezer. To freeze, divide among freezer bags, about 16 ounces (about 2 cups) per bag. To reheat, add a couple scoops of polenta and a splash of milk to a pan. Stir over low heat until it becomes warm. If it looks too thick, add another splash of milk.

GOES WELL WITH:

Smothered Italian Sausage (page 139) • Meltdown Meal

Chicken (or Anything) Milanese (page 142) • Weeknight Meal

A 100% Chance of Meatballs (page 146) • Weeknight Meal

the pot. The polenta will start to thicken. Switch to stirring with a wooden spoon once it has a porridge-like consistency.

3. Cover the pot, offset the lid, and stir frequently, scraping the bottom with the wooden spoon, for about 1 hour.

4. Remove from the heat. Stir in the grated parmesan and salt to taste. Serve immediately.

NOTE: *The exact amount of milk you will need depends on the brand of polenta. Some are more absorbent than others. I'd start with more than you might need, just because it's easy to cook off.*

BREAD AND
THINGS O

N IT

BAKING, IN GENERAL, IS A GREAT WAY TO INVOLVE
kids in cooking. One of the most popular toys of all time is called Play-
Doh precisely because kids love playing with dough. Real dough isn't
that different from the play version. You can mix and knead and roll and
push and pull. Hands get dirty. Mouths start to smile. Food is made and
food is fed.

Of course, the process is just one half of baking. Once baked, bread
becomes an ingenious conveyor, carrying everything from cheese and
sauce (as in pizza) to peanut butter and apple (as in sandwiches) to garlic
and butter (as in garlic bread).

These recipes harness both sides of bread. Some recipes—like the
pizza and focaccia—take time and are best suited for when you have the
luxury to bake at home. Other recipes take advantage of bread's ability to
make a convenient delightful meal out of disparate ingredients. If you
are in the need for sandwiches but not the time to bake for yourself, no
shame in grabbing a loaf of country levain bread and using that.

A BETTER GRILLED CHEESE

2 (1-inch/2.5 cm) thick slices crusty country loaf bread of your choice

2 slices sharp cheddar cheese (1 ounce/30g each)

2 slices provolone cheese (1½ ounces/45g each)

2 tablespoons goat cheese

2 tablespoons (30g) unsalted butter, at room temperature

You'd be hard-pressed to find something that screams ''I've had a tough day, the world's got me down, and I need some comfort!'' more than a grilled cheese. Hopefully that doesn't happen every day, because this recipe is extremely decadent. But at the right moment, this recipe makes you feel immensely cared about. You'll want thick slices of crusty country bread, which give a bit of tangy sourness to the gooey, salty, terrific cheese inside. Also elevating the sandwich is the addition of goat cheese, which adds tang and breaks up the monotony of the provolone and cheddar. It's also a great way to Trojan Horse a new cheese into your kids' repertoire so later, when they're feeling much better and wrinkle their noses up at the idea of goat cheese, you can say, ''Aha! You had it and you liked it!'' And the best part is, all of this can be on the table in less than 30 minutes from walking through the door.

1. Lay the bread on a clean work surface. Put cheddar on one slice and layer the provolone on top of it. Spread the goat cheese evenly on the other slice of bread. Put the sandwich together. Spread half of the softened butter on the outside of one of the sides, coating evenly, edge to edge.

2. Heat a sauté pan over medium-high heat, making sure it doesn't smoke. Place the sandwich in the pan, buttered-side down. (It should sizzle but never smoke.) While the sandwich is in the pan, butter the top slice of bread, edge to edge. Press down on the sandwich with a spatula. Flip after a few minutes and toast the other side. Repeat, pressing and flipping until both the bread is toasted and the cheese is melted.

3. Slice in half and serve immediately.

A BETTER GRILLED CHEESE, *page 226*

SUMMERTIME BAGEL

1 sesame bagel, halved horizontally

2 (1-inch/2.5cm) thick slices very ripe tomato (heirloom or other meaty varietal)

Coarse sea salt

Freshly ground black pepper

4 ounces (115g) cream cheese

Extra-virgin olive oil, with fruity or herbaceous notes (e.g., Sicilian, Ligurian, or California variety)

Toasted sesame seeds

When I was a little kid, I didn't like tomatoes. Or I *thought* I didn't like tomatoes. Then one day during the peak of summer, on a road trip to Yosemite, we stopped at a fruit stand. My dad took a ripe tomato that had been warmed by the sun. He sprinkled some salt on it. It looked plump and firm. It was my nemesis. He asked me to try it. I refused. He asked me again. I refused again. Finally, as I was whining, he shoved it into my protesting mouth. "I hate toma . . ." My mouth was full of this sweet umami-based, acid-spiked, juicy, unbelievably flavorful substance. It was . . . a tomato.

That day my father imparted two bits of wisdom to me. First and foremost, you simply cannot oversalt a perfectly ripe juicy tomato. Second, sometimes—not always, but sometimes—parenting is looking past your child's whims and just deciding for them.

1. Toast the bagel to your desired doneness.

2. On a cutting board, season the tomatoes with coarse salt, edge to edge, so the salt is visible, and black pepper.

3. Divide the cream cheese evenly between the bagel halves and spread thickly. Place a tomato slice on each half. Drizzle some olive oil all over the bagel, so it is dripping off of it. Sprinkle a generous amount of sesame seeds on top. Enjoy immediately.

PESTO GRILLED CHICKEN SANDOS

2 (4 × 6-inch/10 × 15cm) rectangles focaccia (page 231)

2 Save Your Ass Grilled Chicken breasts (page 137)

½ cup (135g) basil pesto (from Basil Pesto Pasta, page 96)

¼ red onion, thinly sliced

5 pepperoncini, sliced

1 tablespoon brine from the jar of pepperoncini

1 (467g) jar marinated artichoke hearts, roughly chopped

1 tablespoon extra-virgin olive oil

Pinch of kosher salt

A few turns of freshly ground black pepper

8 slices provolone cheese

Preparing these over-the-top sandwiches is formidable at first blush. But if you make the pesto and focaccia the night before, and you've followed my advice to keep some Save Your Ass Grilled Chicken (page 137) in the fridge, it's just assembly. (And look, you can use store-bought focaccia and even store-bought pesto, if you want. Then it's just *buying* and assembly.) Every flavor here is maximized: Well-spiced chicken. Fresh basil pesto. I like the pickled heat of pepperoncini (with their liquid) and artichokes. But you can freestyle as you see fit. The overall idea is maximum flavor with the least amount of work possible.

1. Preheat the oven to 400°F (200°C).

2. Place the focaccia on a sheet pan, bottom-side up, and toast until the underside is crispy, about 10 minutes. Remove from the oven and set aside. Leave the oven on.

3. Thinly slice the chicken and place in a small bowl. Add the pesto and toss to coat the chicken evenly.

4. In another bowl, combine the onion, pepperoncini, pepperoncini brine, artichoke hearts, olive oil, salt, and pepper. Toss until the vegetables are well coated. Set aside.

5. Slice both pieces of focaccia in half horizontally. Working with one sandwich at a time, spoon half of the pesto chicken

RECIPE CONTINUES

onto the bottom half of the focaccia. Place 2 slices of provolone on top of the chicken and the other 2 on the top of half of the focaccia. Repeat with the other piece of focaccia.

6. Line a sheet pan with foil and grease lightly with olive oil. Place the sandwiches on the sheet pan and bake until the cheese is melted and slightly browned, 5 to 7 minutes.

7. Remove from the oven. Top with the vegetable mixture and put the sandwiches together. Slice in half to serve.

PEANUT BUTTER APPLE TOAST, HONEY, AND DUKKAH

MELTDOWN MEAL

1 (1-inch/2.5cm) thick slice country levain bread or other nice bread

2 tablespoons peanut butter

½ apple, thinly sliced

1½ teaspoons honey, preferably local

2 teaspoons Dukkah (page 18); see Notes

NOTES:

- *The size of your bread will change how much of the toppings you will use and vice versa.*

- *If dukkah isn't something you want to make, substitute with a couple of your favorite nuts instead.*

A year after Helena was born, I lived in a tiny one-bedroom apartment near my restaurant. On the way to the farmers' market, every morning, I'd bring her with me to a little store called Yo Tambien Cantina—a tiny cafe run by Kenzie Benesh and Isabella Bertorelli—for coffee and tamales. They used to serve something very similar to this: peanut butter, apples, and honey on toast topped with dukkah, the wonderfully nutty Egyptian spice mix. Helena, my dog, Cassidy, and I would sit in the park, where Helena would happily pick off the apples and chew them while Cassidy waited for crumbs to drop. Now when Helena and I make this in the mornings, or after school, she happily eats the whole thing and I remember those early days fondly.

Not only can your kid help you make this sandwich, they can make it themselves, too. Just supervise the application of the honey.

1. Toast the bread to your desired level of doneness.

2. Spread the peanut butter onto the toast. Overlap the apple slices on top of the peanut butter. Drizzle honey on top of the apple. Sprinkle the dukkah on top of the honey and enjoy.

GARLIC BREAD

1 stick (4 ounces/115g) unsalted butter

18 garlic cloves, peeled but whole

1 sprig fresh rosemary, leaves picked and chopped

⅓ cup (10g) packed fresh Italian parsley leaves

1 teaspoon (3g) kosher salt

¼ cup (5g) packed fresh basil leaves

2 pinches of chile flakes (optional)

1 loaf Italian country bread or French bread, halved horizontally

8 ounces (225g) low-moisture mozzarella cheese, thinly sliced

6 tablespoons freshly grated Parmigiano-Reggiano cheese

This is a great way of subverting your children's will and getting them to eat something green and herbaceous that is not threatening.

Cheesy garlic bread is about as nostalgic as you can get for me, but it's also filled with a ton of herbs, delivering something aromatic and green.

1. Preheat the oven to 375°F (190°C).

2. In a small saucepan, combine the butter and garlic and heat over medium heat. After 10 minutes, add the rosemary and cook until the garlic is lightly browned but the butter is not, about 2 minutes. Remove from the heat.

There are a lot of herbs to pick here. Great work for small hands.

3. Pour the butter/garlic mixture into a food processor and add the parsley, salt, basil, and chile flakes (if using), and puree.

4. Using a rubber spatula, evenly spread the mixture across the bread, from edge to edge but not too thickly (or the bread will be soggy).

5. Lay the sliced mozzarella over the bread. Evenly sprinkle parmesan atop the mozzarella. Set the bread on a baking sheet lined with parchment paper.

6. Transfer to the oven and bake until the cheese is melted and golden brown, about 15 minutes. Remove from the oven and eat piping hot, cut into 2- to 3-inch (5 to 7.5cm) pieces.

THE BEST FOCACCIA OF YOUR LIFE

2 teaspoons (15g) honey

¼ cup (60g) warm water

3 cups (700g) cold water

8 cups (1.2kg) all-purpose flour

1 tablespoon plus about
1 teaspoon (12g) active dry yeast

1 tablespoon (5g) diastatic malt powder

2 tablespoons (27g) fine sea salt

2 cups (400g) extra-virgin olive oil

1 tablespoon (7g) flaky sea salt

1 sprig fresh rosemary (optional), chopped

EQUIPMENT:

Stand mixer

I can think of little else more satisfying than pulling a tray of golden fluffy dimpled focaccia from the oven. But it takes some time and patience to get there. Dough, like children, needs rest. Ample mixing helps a dough build gluten and you don't want to rush this focaccia or the dough will contract on the sheet pan. A few other tricks I've learned to turn this maximally impressive bread into a minimally laborious process: First is diastatic malt powder. Sounds obscure but it isn't. You'll find it at any natural foods store and also—because of course you can find anything there—on the Internet. Here it functions as a sugar that the yeast devours to make it more active and helps the focaccia turn deeply golden. Finally, there's a ton of olive oil in here, so it's even more important than ever to use the highest quality EVOO you can find.

Besides eating it, the great joys of baking focaccia, especially for little helpers, are stretching out the dough and dimpling it with their fingers.

1. In a small bowl, combine the honey and warm water, mixing until the honey is dissolved. Add the cold water.

2. In the bowl of a stand mixer, fitted with the dough hook, combine the flour, yeast, malt powder, and sea salt. Set the speed to low (level 2) and slowly pour in the honey-water, mixing until just combined. Increase the speed to

RECIPE CONTINUES

NOTE: *This can be baked the day before and refreshed in the oven at 375°F (190°C) for 10 minutes before serving.*

medium (level 4) and add ¾ cup (150g) of the olive oil, mixing until fully incorporated. Stop the mixer to scrape the sides and bottom of the bowl with a rubber spatula, then restart the mixer on medium and mix for 10 minutes. Stop the mixer, scrape down the sides and bottom, and return to medium-high (level 6) for 8 minutes. Stop the mixer once more, to scrape down the sides and bottom, and mix again on the highest speed for 30 seconds. Continue, working in 30-second increments, until the dough comes together. (Do not put your mixer on the edge of the counter. It'll jump off.) Scrape down the sides of the bowl. Cover the bowl in plastic wrap and let the dough rest for 40 minutes.

3. Pour ½ cup (100g) of the olive oil on an 18 × 13-inch (46 × 33cm) half-sheet pan and make sure the entire surface is well covered. Place the dough onto the center of the oiled pan. Fold the sides in toward the center. Rotate the pan and simultaneously tuck in the edges while folding/flipping the entire dough in on itself. This will create a smooth top and a seamed bottom. Add some oil to the plastic wrap and cover the pan. Rest for an additional 45 minutes in a warm area.

4. When you're ready to stretch the dough, remove the plastic wrap. With your fingers, stretch the dough from the center out until it covers the entire surface of the sheet pan. Rest for 45 minutes uncovered in a warm place.

5. Make dimples in the dough all over, evenly, pressing your fingers into the dough. Cover with plastic and rest for 1 hour.

6. Preheat the oven to 425°F (220°C).

7. Remove the plastic wrap a final time. Season the focaccia with flaky salt and rosemary (if using). Place the focaccia in the oven. Throw 2 tablespoons water directly inside the oven to create steam and promptly shut the door.

8. Bake until dark golden brown, about 25 minutes.

9. Remove the focaccia from the oven. Pour the remaining ¾ cup (150g) olive oil over it while it is still warm. Let the focaccia rest for 30 minutes before serving.

PIZZA (AND VARIATIONS)

FOR THE PIZZA DOUGH:

3 cups plus 2 tablespoons (500g) bread flour

1 tablespoon (11g) diastatic malt powder

1 tablespoon (15g) kosher salt

½ cup (118g) warm water

1 envelope (7g) active dry yeast

1 tablespoon (25g) honey

1¼ cups (296g) ice water

2 tablespoons (25g) extra-virgin olive oil

FOR SHAPING AND RISING:

All-purpose flour, for the work surface

1 cup (240ml) extra-virgin olive oil

FOR THE TOPPINGS:

See the variations on pages 245 to 251: Cheese Pie, Pepperoni Pizza, and White Pie with Ricotta, Sausage, and Broccolini, or Pizza Rossa

EQUIPMENT:

Stand mixer, bench knife, digital kitchen scale

Watching an experienced pizzaiolo move is like watching a dancer. Making pizza at home is not like this at all—it's a messier, longer, and much more fun process. There is some forethought, of course. For a truly excellent pizza, the dough has to undergo a fermentation process by which the yeast consumes the sugars, spitting out CO_2. This dough can be refrigerated (retarded) overnight if needed (follow the directions below).

Kids have an extra stomach dedicated exclusively to pizza. Especially if they're the ones who helped roll out the dough and sprinkle on the ingredients.

Below is a general dough recipe with cooking instructions, then four of my favorite variations: a classic cheese pie, a pepperoni pie, a white pie, and a cheeseless red pie.

1. In a stand mixer, fitted with the dough hook, mix on low speed (level 2) the flour, malt powder, and salt until just combined. Turn off the mixer. With a rubber spatula, scrape the bottom of the bowl.

2. In a small bowl, combine the warm water, yeast, and honey. Whisk together until the honey and yeast have dissolved. Let sit for 2 to 3 minutes. The surface will become foamy.

3. In another small bowl, combine the ice water and olive oil.

4. Turn the mixer on low speed (level 2) and slowly add the warm honey/yeast mixture. Mix for about 20 seconds.

RECIPE CONTINUES

5. Slowly add the water/oil combination, to different parts of the bowl, to help absorb the flour on the sides. Mix on low (level 2) for about 30 seconds. Stop the mixer and scrape the sides of the bowl with the spatula. Mix on low (2) for 2 minutes.

6. Turn the speed up to medium (level 4) and mix for 20 minutes. By the end the dough should mostly be wrapped around the dough hook and any remaining dough in the bowl should easily pull away from the sides. If, after 20 minutes, the dough is not yet ready, increase the speed to 6 for an additional 30 seconds.

7. Stop the mixer. With wet hands, remove the dough from the hook. It should remove easily and cleanly.

8. To shape and let rise: Lightly flour a clean work surface. Turn the dough out onto the prepared surface, using a plastic bowl scraper. Dust the top of a scale. Weigh the dough (it should be around 900g) and with a bench knife, cut into 2 even portions (about 450g each). Gather the edges of one dough portion and both tuck and fold them toward the center, creating a seamed and smooth side. Flip the dough with the seam-side down and with the knife edge (pinky side) of your hand, rotate the ball counterclockwise between your hands, tucking and smoothing the bottom edges, using the table to create friction and tension. The bottom seam should smooth out. (If it doesn't and there is a gap, simply pinch the seams together like a dumpling.) Repeat with the other dough portion.

9. Oil two 18 × 13-inch (46 × 33cm) half-sheet pans with ½ cup (120ml) olive oil each, making sure the entire surface is oiled. Place 1 ball of dough, seam-side down, in the center of each pan. Lightly oil the top of the dough and loosely cover with plastic wrap. (If not making pizza until the next day, at this point place the dough, covered, in the refrigerator overnight.) Rest at room temperature for 2 hours.

10. Remove the plastic wrap and reserve. Tap your fingertips in the oil on the tray and begin to create dimples in

- *I developed this dough just for this book with the home cook in mind. It is meant to be handled minimally and baked on a metal sheet pan for convenience. This dough is not meant to be stretched in the air and baked in a wood-fired-style oven.*

- *My approach to toppings is to not use too many. You're not making a 4-pound dough shovel. You're making a pizza.*

the dough, from the center out. Carefully place your hands under the dough and gently stretch it toward the edges of the sheet pan. (The dough will not cover the entire pan.) Repeat with the second portion of dough. Cover with the plastic wrap and rest for another 30 minutes.

11. When ready to bake, preheat the oven to 400°F (200°C). Top and bake as directed in the variations.

Make-Ahead Pizza

If you want to freeze your pizzas, the best way to do that is to stretch the dough, brush with olive oil, and parbake—meaning partially bake them—for 15 minutes at 400°F (200°C). Let them cool to room temperature before freezing. When you're ready to cook them, top them with cheese or whatever else and bake for an additional 15 minutes at 400°F (200°C).

CHEESE PIE

Pizza dough (page 243)

1 (28-ounce/794g) can crushed tomatoes

Kosher salt

1 large garlic clove, thinly sliced

1 cup (9 ounces/250g) diced low-moisture mozzarella cheese

1 cup (9 ounces/250g) ricotta cheese

20 fresh basil leaves

2 tablespoons extra-virgin olive oil

½ cup (55g) freshly grated Parmigiano-Reggiano cheese

1. Make the pizza dough as directed through the 2-hour rest, but without shaping yet.

RECIPE CONTINUES

2. Meanwhile, set a fine-mesh sieve over a bowl. Empty the can of crushed tomatoes into the sieve and let drain for 1 hour.

3. While the tomatoes are draining, shape the dough as directed, and let rest for 30 minutes, and preheat the oven to 400°F (200°C).

4. Working with one pizza at a time (and dividing the toppings evenly), dollop the tomatoes evenly over the stretched dough with a large spoon and gently spread

around. Salt the pizza, from edge to edge, with kosher salt. Spread the garlic on top of the sauce.

5. Sprinkle the diced mozzarella over the pizza, making sure to top all the way to the edge so the pizza isn't weighed down in the middle. Drop the ricotta in even spoonfuls over the pizza. Add the basil leaves and drizzle the olive oil over the entire pizza. Edge to edge, sprinkle the parmesan on top. Repeat with the other pizza.

6. Bake each pizza until the crust is deeply golden brown, about 25 minutes. Let sit for 10 minutes before cutting and enjoying.

PEPPERONI PIZZA

2½ ounces (75g) pepperoni

Follow the directions for the Cheese Pie. Add the pepperoni after the ricotta and before the basil leaves.

WHITE PIE WITH RICOTTA, SAUSAGE, AND BROCCOLINI

Pizza dough (page 243)

Kosher salt

½ bunch broccolini (3½ ounces/100g), cut into bite-sized stems and florets

14 ounces (400g) sweet or hot Italian sausage, casings removed

1 large garlic clove, thinly sliced

9 ounces (250g) provolone cheese, shredded (1½ cups)

1 cup (9 ounces/250g) ricotta cheese

20 fresh basil leaves

2 tablespoons (25g) extra-virgin olive oil

½ cup (55g) Parmigiano-Reggiano cheese, grated

Grated zest of 1 lemon

Calabrian chili bomba (optional, see page 293)

RECIPE CONTINUES

1. Make the pizza dough as directed, shaping it on the two sheet pans and giving it its 30-minute rest.

2. Meanwhile, bring a large pot of generously salted water to a rolling boil. Prepare a bowl of ice water and set it next to the stove.

3. Blanch the broccolini for 30 seconds and carefully move to the ice bath with tongs. Once cool, remove the blanched broccolini from the ice bath and wring it out well with your hands. Set aside.

4. Break up the sausage into small pieces and set aside.

5. Preheat the oven to 400°F (200°C).

6. Working with one pizza at a time (and dividing the toppings evenly), salt the pizza, from edge to edge, with kosher salt. Spread the garlic on top of the dough.

7. Sprinkle on the shredded provolone, making sure to top the pizza all the way to the edge so it isn't weighed down in the middle. Drop the ricotta in even spoonfuls over the pizza. Sprinkle the sausage meat over the cheeses. Add half of the blanched broccolini on top of the sausage. Add the basil leaves and drizzle the olive oil over the entire pizza. Edge to edge, sprinkle the parmesan on top. Repeat with the other pizza.

8. Bake each pizza until the crust is deeply golden brown, about 25 minutes. Let sit for 10 minutes. Finish with lemon zest and Calabrian chili bomba (if using) before cutting and serving.

PIZZA ROSSA

Pizza dough (page 243)

1 (28-ounce/794g) can crushed tomatoes

Kosher salt

1 large garlic clove, thinly sliced

RECIPE AND INGREDIENTS CONTINUE

20 fresh basil leaves

2 tablespoons plus ¼ cup (60ml) extra-virgin olive oil

2 tablespoons fresh lemon juice

4 packed cups (3½ ounces/100g) arugula

2½ ounces (70g) oil-packed anchovy fillets (8 to 10)

Pinch of chile flakes

1. Make the pizza dough as directed through the 2-hour rest, but without shaping yet.

2. Meanwhile, set a fine-mesh sieve over a bowl. Empty the can of crushed tomatoes into the sieve and let drain for 1 hour.

3. While the tomatoes are draining, shape the dough as directed, and let rest for 30 minutes, and preheat the oven to 400°F (200°C).

4. Working with one pizza at a time (and dividing the toppings evenly), dollop the tomatoes evenly over the stretched dough with a large spoon and gently spread around. Salt the pizza, from edge to edge, with kosher salt. Spread the garlic on top of the sauce. Add the basil leaves and drizzle 1 tablespoon of the olive oil over the entire pizza. Repeat with the other pizza.

5. Bake each pizza until the crust is deeply golden brown, about 25 minutes.

6. Let sit for 10 minutes.

7. In a small bowl, toss the arugula with the remaining ¼ cup (60ml) olive oil, the lemon juice, and a pinch of salt. Top the rested pizzas with 8 to 10 anchovies each and the dressed arugula. Add a pinch of chile flakes and enjoy immediately.

SNACKS

SWEETS

WHEN IT COMES TO COOKING FOR YOUR KIDS, THIS chapter doesn't require much of a sales pitch. It's not like grains or vegetables or the dreaded salads. Most kids love sweets. Most adults do, too.

Personally, I never baked much—certainly not at home—until I became a single dad. Making brownies, cookies, and cupcakes was a way for me to maximize my time with Helena. The delicious treats, which she would bring to her teachers, were the by-product.

Naturally, as a chef and a dad, I try to find ways to make these desserts more nutritional like using whole-grain stone-milled flour and coconut sugar (blah blah blah), but I'm not pushing it. The only people who crave health food cookies are those who have never had a real one. These are decadent, delicious, fatty, and sweet. After all, everything is good in moderation, including moderation.

Note: I've abandoned the Meltdown Meal, Weeknight Meal, and Project Cooking labels here. No one is making double dark chocolate cookies in the midst of a meltdown. And hopefully no one is thinking of these recipes as an entire meal.

BANANA CHOCOLATE WALNUT BREAD

1 tablespoon (15g) unsalted butter, softened, for the pan

¾ cup (100g) chopped walnuts

4 very ripe bananas

⅓ cup (85g) whole-milk Greek yogurt or full-fat sour cream

6 tablespoons (85g) unsalted butter, melted and cooled

2 teaspoons vanilla extract

2 large eggs

1 cup (190g) packed light or dark brown sugar

Scant 2 cups (235g) all-purpose or whole wheat flour

1½ teaspoons (9g) baking soda

½ teaspoon (3g) fine sea salt

¾ cup (135g) dark chocolate chips

1 tablespoon turbinado sugar, for finishing

EQUIPMENT:

9 × 5-inch (23 × 13cm) loaf pan

A banana is a delicate thing indeed and sometimes you end up with a whole cluster of soft, mushy, brown ones. But brown is not the end of a banana, just the beginning of a new stage in its life. As soon as one darkens to the point of avoidance, I'll peel it, put it in a ziplock bag, and freeze it. These bananas find later use in smoothies and, when we have time, this banana chocolate walnut bread. Smoothies are fast and nutritious; banana bread is easy and delicious. We generally bake at night, let it cool, and, in the morning, everyone gets a slice.

1. Preheat the oven to 375°F (190°C). Grease a 9 × 5-inch (23 × 13cm) loaf pan with 1 tablespoon of softened butter.

2. In a dry sauté pan, toast the walnuts over medium-high heat, stirring occasionally to avoid burning. Once fragrant, 5 to 6 minutes, remove them from the pan and set aside to cool.

3. In a large bowl, mash the bananas with a fork, leaving some lumpy parts. Add the yogurt, melted butter, vanilla, eggs, and brown sugar and mix to combine.

4. In a small bowl, combine the flour, baking soda, and salt.

5. Add the flour mixture to the banana mixture using a rubber spatula, combining until

Making banana bread is a group activity. Kids can mix, break eggs, whisk, and pour, helping nearly every step of the way.

RECIPE CONTINUES

incorporated, being careful not to overmix. Fold in ⅔ cup (90g) of the chocolate chips and ½ cup (60g) of the walnuts, reserving the remaining chocolate and nuts for topping

6. Pour the batter into the prepared pan, tapping the pan on the counter to make sure the mixture is even and flat. Sprinkle the remaining chocolate and walnuts on top, followed by the turbinado sugar. Place the filled loaf pan on a sheet pan.

7. Bake until the loaf starts pulling away from the sides of the pan, 1 hour to 1 hour 15 minutes.

8. Let the loaf cool for 30 minutes in the pan, then turn it out of the pan to cool for an additional 30 minutes before cutting and serving.

NOTE: *If using frozen bananas, microwave them just a bit to soften unless you remember to pull them out of the freezer and into the fridge a day in advance. Then drain off the liquid (if any) before you use them.*

BUTTERMILK CORNBREAD

1 tablespoon (15g) unsalted butter, softened, for the baking dish

14½ ounces (412g) unsalted butter

1½ cups (230g) coarsely ground cornmeal

1½ cups (220g) all-purpose or (preferably) whole wheat flour

½ cup (100g) packed light or dark brown sugar

1 tablespoon (9g) kosher salt

1½ tablespoons (15g) baking powder

1½ teaspoons (7g) baking soda

1 cup (250ml) buttermilk

1 (16-ounce/455g) container sour cream

4 large eggs (240g total)

FOR SERVING:

Softened butter

Honey

Flaky sea salt

I'm a child of KFC's and Popeye's cornbread and didn't have the homemade stuff until family meal at Eleven Madison Park. The reasons it became a staff favorite there are the same reasons I love making it at home and why Helena's eyes light up. It's quick. There's little work involved. It is versatile, meaning, it goes as well with some butter and jam as it does with a bowl of chili. And the texture—thanks to the sour cream and buttermilk—is the perfect balance of crumbly and supple.

1. Preheat the oven to 425°F (220°C). Liberally grease a 9 × 13-inch (23 × 33cm) baking dish on all sides with 1 tablespoon softened butter.

2. In a small saucepan, melt the butter over high heat. Once the butter is melted and starts bubbling, reduce the heat to medium. There's no need to stir, but keep an eye on it for 4 to 5 minutes. Once the butter has a nutty aroma and the sides of the pan start to brown, whisk to encourage even browning and incorporate the milk solids from the sides of the pan into the mixture. When the butter is light brown and the flavor is nutty, remove from the heat completely, continuing to whisk for a few seconds. Set aside and cool to room temperature.

3. Meanwhile, in a large bowl, combine the cornmeal, flour, brown sugar, salt, baking powder, and baking soda. Whisk together.

RECIPE CONTINUES

4. Once cooled, pour 1 cup (225g) of the brown butter into a spouted measuring cup. Pour the remaining generous ¾ cup (185g) brown butter into a small bowl and set aside. For both amounts, make sure you incorporate as much of the browned milk solids off the side of the pot as possible.

5. In a second large bowl, whisk the buttermilk, sour cream, and eggs. Pour in the 1 cup brown butter and whisk until incorporated.

6. Add half of the wet ingredients to the flour mixture and slowly whisk, being careful not to overmix. Add the rest of the wet ingredients, scraping the bowl down with a rubber spatula. Continue to fold together slowly with the spatula, scraping from the bottom of the bowl to eliminate any unmixed pockets of dry ingredients. Pour the batter into the prepared pan and spread evenly.

7. Bake until a fork or toothpick comes out clean, 20 to 25 minutes. If you tap the center, it should have a hollow sound and it won't jiggle.

8. Let the cornbread sit for 15 minutes, then brush with the reserved brown butter. Slice into pieces.

9. Serve with additional softened butter, honey, and a pinch of coarse or flaky salt.

PEANUT BUTTER BROWNIES

Softened unsalted butter,
for the pan

Scant 2 cups (12 ounces/340g)
dark chocolate chips

6 tablespoons (85g) unsalted
butter

¼ cup (20g) cocoa powder

¼ cup (50g) extra-virgin olive oil

1 cup (200g) brown sugar or
coconut sugar

3 large eggs (180g)

1 tablespoon (12g) vanilla extract

¾ cup (100g) whole wheat flour

1 teaspoon (3g) kosher salt

7 tablespoons (4 ounces/115g)
peanut butter

¼ teaspoon flaky sea salt,
to finish

EQUIPMENT:

8 × 8-inch (20 × 20cm) baking pan

I vividly remember when I began to bake with Helena. The end result—cookies, cakes, brownies—were sweet but not nearly as sweet as the experience of working side by side. These comforting brownies come from that time, when I was looking for ways to engage with her. I just wanted to be near her so badly. She loved mixing the batter, glopping on the peanut butter and then the chocolate chips and, of course, licking the spatula. More than anything, though, she loved eating them.

This recipe is best made with a child, as the only thing sweeter than the brownies is watching them whisk, mix, and glop.

1. Preheat the oven to 350°F (180°C). Grease an 8 × 8-inch (20 × 20cm) baking pan with butter.

2. In a microwave-safe bowl, combine ¾ cup (170g) of the chocolate chips and the butter. Microwave for 1 minute. Add the cocoa powder and whisk until incorporated and shiny.

3. Add the olive oil to the melted chocolate and whisk until smooth. Add the brown sugar, eggs, and vanilla and whisk until combined. Add the flour and kosher salt and whisk constantly for 30 seconds.

4. Using a rubber spatula, scrape the brownie batter into the baking pan. Spread until level. Tap the pan on the counter.

RECIPE CONTINUES

5. Add the peanut butter and remaining chocolate chips to the top of the batter. Use a fork to spread evenly over the surface (see Note).

6. Bake until set on the edges and slightly pulling away from the sides, about 30 minutes.

7. Sprinkle the top with flaky salt. Let cool for 30 minutes before serving.

NOTE: *If your peanut butter is resistant to spreading, soften it in a microwave-safe bowl for 15 to 20 seconds.*

CUPPYCAKES WITH VANILLA BUTTERCREAM FROSTING

1¼ cups (175g) whole wheat pastry flour

1¼ teaspoons (3g) baking powder

1 teaspoon (5g) baking soda

½ teaspoon kosher salt

8 tablespoons (4 ounces/115g) unsalted butter, at room temperature

¾ cup and about 3 tablespoons (185g) granulated sugar

2 large eggs (120g total)

2 teaspoons vanilla extract

½ cup (120ml) buttermilk

¾ cup (180g) sour cream

Vanilla Buttercream Frosting (recipe follows)

EQUIPMENT:

Stand mixer (or hand mixer), muffin tin, #10 (3-ounce) ice cream scoop

We use whole wheat flour here. The texture is so light yet it has integrity. It's a good example of a small modification that hardly affects flavor but gets more nutrients into your kid.

I still get emotional when thinking about making cuppycakes with Helena. This was our first bake together. In fact, she has a version of this recipe written down in her own recipe book. You can either make the cuppycakes and frosting all at once or, and this is what I'd recommend, make the frosting ahead of time and keep it in the fridge until you're ready to frost.

1. Preheat the oven to 350°F (180°C). Line 12 cups of a muffin tin with cupcake liners.

2. In a bowl, whisk together the flour, baking powder, baking soda, and salt.

3. In a stand mixer fitted with the paddle (or in a large bowl with a handheld mixer), cream together the butter and sugar on medium-high (level 6) until fully combined and light and fluffy, about 5 minutes. Turn off the mixer and scrape down the sides of the bowl with a rubber spatula. Add the eggs and vanilla and mix for an additional 1 minute.

4. Alternate adding the flour mixture and the buttermilk in three additions, beginning and ending with the flour mixture. Once all the dry ingredients and buttermilk have been incorporated, turn off the mixer and scrape down the sides as needed. Remove the bowl from the mixer and, with the spatula, fold in the sour cream until combined without streaks.

RECIPE CONTINUES

If you're making these for a bake sale or birthday party the next day, then bake the cupcakes and let them rest, covered, on the counter overnight. Frost them as close to serving as possible.

5. Use a #10 (3-ounce) ice cream scoop to transfer the batter into the cupcake liners, evenly distributing it among the cups. They should be about two-thirds full.

6. Bake until a toothpick inserted in a cupcake comes out clean, 21 to 23 minutes.

7. Let the cupcakes cool in the pan for 10 minutes, then transfer to a wire rack to cool completely before frosting.

8. Frost the cupcakes with the vanilla buttercream frosting.

VANILLA BUTTERCREAM FROSTING

YIELD: MAKES ENOUGH FOR 12 CUPCAKES

1½ cups (350ml) heavy cream

1 tablespoon vanilla extract

8 ounces (225g) cream cheese, at room temperature

2 cups (235g) powdered sugar

4 tablespoons (55g) unsalted butter, at room temperature

1. In a bowl, whisk the heavy cream and vanilla until medium peaks form, being careful not to overmix.

2. In another bowl, stir the softened cream cheese, powdered sugar, and butter together with a wooden spoon until creamy and combined.

3. With a rubber spatula, gently fold the whipped cream mixture into the cream cheese mixture in thirds.

4. Transfer the frosting to a pastry bag with a fluted tip for decorating. You may also keep in the bowl and use an offset spatula to spread the frosting onto the cupcakes. Refrigerate the frosting (either in the pastry bag or covered in the bowl) for 1 hour before using.

CHOCOLATE CAKE WITH CHOCOLATE BUTTERCREAM FROSTING

Softened butter and flour, for the pans

2 cups (210g) whole wheat pastry or cake flour

1¾ cups (350g) granulated sugar

1 cup (80g) unsweetened Dutch-process cocoa powder

2 teaspoons (8g) baking powder

2 teaspoons (12g) baking soda

1 teaspoon (3g) kosher salt

1 teaspoon (2g) espresso powder

1 cup (225g) buttermilk

½ cup (105g) extra-virgin olive oil

2 large eggs (120g total)

1 tablespoon (14g) vanilla extract

1 cup (250ml) boiling water

Chocolate Buttercream Frosting (recipe follows)

Sprinkles, to finish

EQUIPMENT:

Stand mixer (or hand mixer)

I am not a natural baker—I break too many rules in the kitchen—nor am I a cake lover. But when your daughter asks to make cake with you, there's only one answer: You make cake. And for me, I wanted to make the most decadent, delicious, and flavorful cake I could. I don't know enough about baking to know *why* this version is so moist and supple—though I'd wager it has to do with the generous amount of fat in the cake in the form of olive oil and buttermilk—but it is, without a doubt, a winner.

While you might question giving a five-year-old espresso powder, this little doesn't make them bounce off the walls, at least no more than a slice of chocolate cake normally would.

1. **Stand mixer (or hand mixer)** Preheat the oven to 350°F (180°C). Butter and lightly flour two 9-inch (23cm) round cake pans.

2. In a stand mixer fitted with the paddle (or in a large bowl with a whisk), whisk together the flour, sugar, cocoa powder, baking powder, baking soda, salt, and espresso powder until well combined.

3. Add the buttermilk, olive oil, eggs, and vanilla and mix together on medium speed until well combined. Reduce the speed and carefully add the boiling water to the cake batter until well combined. (The batter will appear very thin at this point.)

RECIPE CONTINUES

4. Divide the cake batter evenly between the two cake pans.

5. Bake until a toothpick or cake tester inserted in the center of one layer comes out clean, 30 to 32 minutes. Be careful not to overbake as this will result in a drier cake.

6. Let the cakes cool in the pans for about 10 minutes, then turn out onto a wire rack to cool completely before frosting.

7. On a cake stand or a plate, place one of the cake layers upside down so the flat side is up. With a spatula, evenly spread 2 cups (480g) of the buttercream on top of the cake. Place the other layer, flat-side down, on top of the frosted layer. Frost the cake with the rest of the buttercream. Decorate with your favorite sprinkles, cut, and serve.

CHOCOLATE BUTTERCREAM FROSTING

YIELD: MAKES ENOUGH FOR ONE 9-INCH (23CM) LAYER CAKE OR 12 CUPCAKES

4 sticks (1 pound/455g) unsalted butter, at room temperature

1½ cups (115g) Dutch-process cocoa powder

5 cups (576g) powdered sugar

¾ cup (180g) whole milk

1 tablespoon (12g) vanilla extract

½ teaspoon espresso powder

NOTE: *If the frosting appears too dry, add more milk, 1 tablespoon at a time, until it reaches the right consistency. If it appears too wet and does not hold its form, add more powdered sugar, 1 tablespoon at a time.*

In a stand mixer (or in a large bowl with a hand mixer), cream the butter and cocoa powder together on medium speed (level 4) until well combined. Add 1 cup (115g) of the powdered sugar and 1 tablespoon of the milk and beat on medium-high (level 6) for about 1 minute. Repeat, alternating with the remaining sugar and milk. Turn the mixer off. Add the vanilla and espresso powder. Turn the mixer to low speed to combine.

BROWN BUTTER CHOCOLATE CHIP OATMEAL COOKIES

2 sticks (8 ounces/225g) unsalted butter

1¼ cups (190g) packed brown sugar

1 tablespoon (10g) vanilla extract

2 large eggs (120g total)

2 cups (315g) whole wheat flour

1 teaspoon (5g) baking soda

2 teaspoons (10g) kosher salt

2 cups (200g) rolled oats

Scant 1½ cups (8½ ounces/240g) dark chocolate chips

¼ teaspoon flaky sea salt, to finish

EQUIPMENT:

#10 (3-ounce) ice cream scoop

If you are a single dad and you are desperately trying to get into the good graces of your child's teachers, I highly recommend bringing these decadent cookies to school. Selfishly, I like to get rid of these as soon as possible or else I'll just end up eating all of them.

1. Preheat the oven to 350°F (180°C). Line a sheet pan with parchment paper.

2. In a small saucepan, melt the butter over high heat. Allow the butter to take on a chestnut brown color, 4 to 5 minutes. Turn off the heat and allow to cool for 5 minutes.

3. In a medium bowl, vigorously whisk the cooled butter together with the brown sugar, vanilla, and eggs until the color lightens and the consistency becomes creamy, about 1 minute.

4. In a separate bowl, sift together the flour, baking soda, and salt.

5. Stir the flour mixture into the egg/butter mixture with a rubber spatula and then fold in the oats and chocolate chips.

6. Using a #10 (3-ounce) ice cream scoop, portion the cookies, then roll them into balls. Place them on the lined sheet pan about 2 inches apart.

RECIPE CONTINUES

7. Bake for 8 minutes. Rotate the pan front to back and bake until lightly golden, an additional 3 minutes.

8. Remove the cookies from the oven and sprinkle the sea salt on top. Let sit for 10 minutes, then serve.

NOTE: *Cookie dough can be scooped and frozen. When you want to bake the cookies, set them out on a lined sheet pan for 20 minutes at room temperature or in the fridge.*

DOUBLE DARK CHOCOLATE COOKIES

2 sticks (8 ounces/225g) unsalted butter, at room temperature

2 cups (390g) brown sugar

2 eggs (120g total)

2 teaspoons (8g) vanilla extract

1⅓ cups (110g) unsweetened Dutch-process cocoa powder

2 cups (250g) whole wheat or all-purpose flour

2 teaspoons (8g) baking powder

1 teaspoon (3g) kosher salt

2½ cups (450g) dark chocolate chips

1 teaspoon (2g) flaky sea salt, to finish

EQUIPMENT:

#10 (3-ounce) ice cream scoop

Hand mixer

This is 100 percent a Helena Nayfeld creation, born one day after hours of shifting desires. (I want them dark; I want them with oats; I want them with dried cherries; I want sprinkles.) Eventually we landed on this decadent recipe, chocolate on chocolate on chocolate. My view on baking cookies, generally, is that the fun is in making them.

1. Preheat the oven to 350°F (180°C). Line a sheet pan with parchment paper.

2. In a large bowl, cream the butter and sugar together at a low speed with a hand mixer, or whisk by hand, until well combined.

3. Add the eggs and vanilla to the bowl. Whisk together on medium speed until creamy and smooth. Add the cocoa powder and whisk to fully incorporate, first on a low speed then increasing once the cocoa is incorporated.

4. In another bowl, mix together the flour, baking powder, and salt.

Sifting, mixing, whisking, scooping, these are all activities kids love.

5. Add the flour mixture to the wet mixture and whisk until the dough comes together, starting on low and slowly increasing to medium, no more than 10 to 15 seconds. Stir in the chocolate chips.

6. Using a #10 (3-ounce) ice cream scoop, portion the cookies onto the lined sheet pan, making sure they are evenly spaced.

7. Bake the cookies for 12 minutes.

8. Remove from the oven, sprinkle with sea salt, and let sit for 5 minutes before serving.

NOTE: *Cookie dough can be scooped and frozen. When you want to bake the cookies, set them out on a lined sheet pan for 20 minutes at room temperature or in the fridge.*

DUTCH APPLE PIE

FOR THE PIE CRUST:

2½ cups (375g) all-purpose flour, plus more for dusting

½ teaspoon (1g) kosher salt

3 tablespoons (40g) granulated cane sugar

2 sticks (8 ounces/225g) unsalted butter, cubed and frozen

4 tablespoons (60g) ice water

1 egg (60g), whisked

FOR THE FILLING:

3½ pounds (1.6kg) small Granny Smith and Gala apples (equal mixture of the two) or other small tart apple varieties, peeled and cut into slices ¼ inch (6mm) thick

2 teaspoons ground cinnamon

1 cup (200g) granulated cane sugar

3 tablespoons all-purpose flour

1½ teaspoons (5g) kosher salt

8 tablespoons (4 ounces/115g) unsalted butter

FOR THE CRUMBLE:

1 cup (160g) all-purpose flour

⅓ cup (65g) packed dark brown sugar

¼ teaspoon ground cinnamon

For my émigré parents, McDonald's (along with Coca-Cola and Levi's) was a symbol of freedom. For me, it was where I could get a twenty-piece chicken nugget meal, fries, and an apple pie. I still crave that gooey cinnamon-y sickly sweet apple filling. As of right now, I do not allow Helena to go to McDonald's, but even I know those days are numbered. In the meantime, we make this delicious Dutch apple pie at home so when she finally does go to Mickey D's, she'll say, "My dad's is better." The final step here is crucial: Some really good vanilla bean ice cream.

1. **Make the pie crust:** In a food processor, combine the flour, salt, and cane sugar and pulse quickly to mix. Add the frozen butter and pulse until the flour and butter create small, pea-sized pieces. (The frozen butter is the secret to a flaky crust.)

2. Add the ice water and egg and mix quickly until just combined, being careful not to overmix. The mixture should still look crumbly, but when pinched between two fingers, it should come together.

3. Remove the dough from the food processor and place in a clean, dry bowl. Knead the dough with your hands until just combined, being careful not to overwork it. It will feel dry but will come together in a few minutes. Knead for an additional 10 to 15 seconds, working quickly so as to not warm the dough too much. Shape the dough into a flat disk

RECIPE AND INGREDIENTS CONTINUE

1 teaspoon (4g) coarse sea salt

½ cup (70g) chopped pecans

8 tablespoons (4 ounces/115g) unsalted butter, at room temperature

FOR SERVING:

Some really good vanilla bean ice cream

EQUIPMENT:

11-inch (28cm) pie plate (2 inches/5cm deep)

about 1½ inches (4cm) thick. Wrap it in plastic wrap and rest in the refrigerator for at least 30 minutes.

4. Make the filling: In a large bowl, toss the apples with the cinnamon, cane sugar, flour, and salt until well coated.

5. In a large pot, melt the butter over high heat. Once melted, add the spiced apples and cook over high heat, stirring occasionally, until the sugar melts and granules are no longer visible, 8 to 10 minutes.

6. Add ½ cup (120ml) water. Bring to a simmer and then reduce the heat to medium. Cook until the sauce thickens, 30 to 35 minutes, stirring occasionally. Once done, set aside to cool completely.

7. Make the crumble: In a small bowl, toss together the flour, brown sugar, cinnamon, salt, pecans, and butter until well combined.

8. Once the pie dough has chilled for 30 minutes, remove it from the refrigerator. Lightly dust a clean work surface with some flour. Dust the top of the dough with a little flour. Press the dough down with your hands and make sure all sides are floured. Working quickly, roll the dough out with a rolling pin from the center out, to maintain a circular shape. If the edges crack, press them back together. Roll until the circle is about 15 inches (38cm) in diameter and about ⅛ inch (3mm) thick.

9. Fold the dough in quarters and transfer to the center of an 11-inch (28cm) deep-dish pie plate and unfold. Press the dough into the pie plate, making sure there are no gaps, and try not to crack the dough. Use a knife to trim the excess edges to run flush with the pie plate. Set in the fridge and rest for 30 minutes.

10. Preheat the oven to 375°F (190°C). Place a sheet pan on the bottom rack to catch any drips.

RECIPE CONTINUES

11. Pour the cooled filling into the pie shell, pressing the apples into the pan. Scatter the crumble evenly over the apples, covering completely. Cover the pie with foil.

12. Bake for 30 minutes. Remove the foil and bake until the edges are golden, about 30 minutes longer.

13. Let the pie rest for at least 30 minutes before serving with some really good vanilla ice cream.

NOTE: *If you want to make the filling ahead of time, make sure that you bring it to room temperature before building and baking the pie.*

STRAWBERRY RHUBARB CAKE

FOR THE FRUIT FILLING:

2 pounds (900g) strawberries, hulled and quartered

1½ pounds (680g) rhubarb, cut into ½-inch slices (6 cups)

¾ cup (150g) granulated sugar

½ cup (60g) all-purpose flour

FOR THE TOPPING:

12 tablespoons (6 ounces/170g) unsalted butter, melted

½ cup (100g) packed light brown sugar

¾ teaspoon vanilla extract

Pinch of kosher salt

1¾ cups (220g) all-purpose flour

1 tablespoon cornstarch (if needed)

FOR THE CAKE BATTER:

Softened unsalted butter, for the baking pan

12 tablespoons (6 ounces/170g) unsalted butter, at room temperature

1 cup (200g) granulated sugar

3 large eggs (180g total)

1¼ cups (240g) sour cream

Grated zest of 1 lemon

1½ teaspoons vanilla extract

When I was growing up, there were always old Russian women living with us. Women my parents brought over from the USSR to take care of my brother and me while they were at work (which was always). Each brought her own food. Some were Belarussian, some Georgian, some Uzbeki. But they all made delicious fruit cakes. There was but one batter for this cake, a fluffy light one into which they'd work the fruit. Later my mother remarried a lovely widower named Edik, who also carried the torch of the preserves and the baking of fruit cakes. This cake is a tribute to them all. Here I use strawberries and rhubarb, a classic combination. You could just as easily use apples, pears, or cherries. Just keep in mind that if the fruit is too wet or juicy, you'll want to add in a tablespoon of cornstarch to tighten it up before it goes on top of the batter.

1. **Make the fruit filling:** In a large bowl, stir together the strawberries, rhubarb, sugar, and flour. Set aside.

2. **Make the topping:** In a small bowl, combine the melted butter, brown sugar, vanilla, salt, and flour and mix until fully incorporated. The texture should be crumbly. Set aside.

3. Preheat the oven to 350°F (180°C). Generously grease a 13 × 9-inch (33 × 23cm) baking pan with butter.

4. **Make the cake batter:** In a stand mixer fitted with the whisk (or in a large bowl with a hand mixer), beat the melted

RECIPE AND INGREDIENTS CONTINUE

1¾ cups (220g) all-purpose flour

1½ teaspoons (6g) baking powder

¾ teaspoon (4g) baking soda

¾ teaspoon kosher salt

EQUIPMENT:

13 × 9-inch (33 × 23cm) baking pan, stand mixer (or hand mixer)

butter and granulated sugar on high for 5 minutes until fluffy. Beat in the eggs, one at a time, until well mixed. Add the sour cream, lemon zest, and vanilla.

5. In a separate bowl, sift together the flour, baking powder, baking soda, and salt. Add the flour mixture to the wet ingredients. Mix until just incorporated, taking care not to overmix. The edges of the bowl should be clean.

6. Add the cake batter to the prepared baking pan. Stir the cornstarch into the fruit filling if it looks too thin. Evenly spread the fruit filling on top. Sprinkle the crumble atop the fruit.

7. Bake until a fork comes out clean, about 1 hour 10 minutes. Let the cake cool on a wire rack for 30 minutes. Slice and enjoy.

STORAGE: Let cool, then store in an airtight container. It'll last up to 3 days on the counter or, in the refrigerator, up to 1 week.

BANOFFEE PIE

3 large bananas (1 pound 6 ounces/625g total), sliced ¼ inch (6mm) thick

1 teaspoon plus 1 tablespoon vanilla extract

Juice of 1 lemon (2 tablespoons/30g)

9½ ounces (275g) graham crackers (about 18)

1 tablespoon (15g) coarse sea salt

Dulce de Leche (page 287); see Note

2 cups (500ml) heavy cream, chilled

3 tablespoons powdered sugar

1 teaspoon ground coffee

About 1 ounce dark chocolate (70% cacao or higher)

EQUIPMENT:

Stand mixer (or hand mixer)

Banana + dulce de leche + whipped cream + graham crackers = banoffee pie. This classic no-bake British dessert is a banger. It's also quick and almost obscenely easy to make, easy to clean up, and keeps well. This version is a little saltier than others you might find, not only because both Helena and I are salt fiends, but because the salt balances out the sweetness, giving each bite a burst of flavor.

Like with the lasagna (page 113), kids love layering this pie. Unlike in the lasagna, be watchful they don't end up eating the whole thing before they're done building it.

1. In a large bowl, toss together the bananas, 1 teaspoon of the vanilla, and the lemon juice.

2. Place the graham crackers in another bowl. Add the sea salt. Break up the crackers with a wooden spoon. It should look like broken cookies rather than cookie dust. (Alternatively, you can put graham crackers and salt in a plastic freezer bag and pound with a mallet.)

3. Place half of the graham cracker crumble into an 8 × 10 × 2½-inch (20 × 25 × 6.5cm) glass serving dish. Add the dulce de leche and mix together with a rubber spatula, then spread evenly in one layer. Top with the bananas in an even layer. Add the rest of the graham cracker crumble on top. Set aside.

RECIPE CONTINUES

NOTE: *If you made the dulce de leche ahead of time and it has been refrigerated, gently warm to room temperature and until loosened.*

4. In a stand mixer fitted with the whisk (or in a bowl with a hand mixer), combine the heavy cream, powdered sugar, ground coffee, and remaining 1 tablespoon vanilla. Whip until stiff peaks form.

5. Spread the whipped cream evenly on top of the graham cracker crumble.

6. Grate dark chocolate over the top of the whipped cream. Refrigerate for 30 minutes and then serve.

DULCE DE LECHE

2 (14-ounce/397g) cans
sweetened condensed milk

In terms of effort-to-reward ratio, dulce de leche is a no-brainer. All you have to do is pop the condensed milk in the oven, set a timer, and a few hours later, a sweet versatile condiment emerges. Dip cookies, apples, or strawberries in it. Pour it over a scoop of ice cream, or olive oil cake, or pound cake. Spoon a little bit out with a pinch of sea salt or dissolve it into a cup of warm milk at night.

Most methods call for boiling the can. I think that works super well, and if you like that way, then do it! It can also be super scary for people who haven't done it before and also really requires you to keep your eye on the water level to avoid a really unpleasant experience.

1. Preheat the oven to 425°F (220°C).

2. Pour the sweetened condensed milk into a 9-inch pie pan and cover tightly with aluminum foil.

3. Set the pie pan in a large baking dish. Pour hot water into the baking dish until it reaches at least halfway up the sides of the pie pan.

4. Place in the oven for 1½ hours.

5. Remove carefully from the oven and let cool for 30 minutes before removing the foil.

STORAGE: Let cool, then store in an airtight container for up to 3 months in the refrigerator.

Setting Up Your Kitchen

When I was coming up in professional kitchens, pots and pans were just tools. They weren't cute. They weren't colorful. Now my Instagram feed is full of cobalt blue rondeaus and oxblood sauciers. Great. You can certainly go down the path of kitchen equipment as lifestyle objects. There are some very nice options out there.

But as for me, I'm a functional guy. I care about size, as it pertains to how much I can cook at one time, and quality, in terms of how the pots and pans retain their heat and how evenly they cook. I also care about space, as in, not wasting it with unnecessary or single-use equipment.

If you have access to, and the means to afford shopping at, a place like Williams-Sonoma, go there. It's one of the few stores in the United States that consistently delivers excellent quality cooking products. But, if you're not able to afford that level of posh, a sneaky hack is to go shop at restaurant supply stores or shop online at webstaurant.com. The equipment is priced for perpetually financially stressed restaurant people. They're not trying to sell you stuff. (Stores that aren't trying to sell you stuff are the best kind of stores.) Especially if you're cooking for larger groups—and in need of larger format sauté pans or stockpots—you can get some pretty steep discounts.

I'm certainly in the camp of if you don't need it, don't have it. But I have also learned that a well–thought out and well-considered battery of kitchen equipment can make cooking not only much easier but much more enjoyable, too. Just as an electrician needs his tools, so, too, does a cook.

PANS AND SKILLETS

You can spend a fortune on pots and pans and if you have a fortune to spend, do it. But you don't have to. For under $300 you can get everything you need—a large cast-iron skillet, a medium cast-iron skillet, two nonstick sauté pans (12-inch/30cm and 8-inch/20cm)—and be able to make everything in this book.

Though more affordable than stainless steel, cast iron takes some coaxing. It's not as simple as washing and putting back in the drawer. But when taken care of, cast iron lasts forever. And even when they're mistreated, they spring back to life with care. I've found some amazing cast-iron pans in thrift and vintage stores.

While a stainless steel or cast-iron pot lasts forever, that's not the case for nonstick pans. Nonsticks are not meant to last forever. As soon as the surface is scratched, it's time to get a new one. That's why I never use metal utensils with a nonstick pan.

A REALLY BIG STOCKPOT

A 20-quart stockpot fits a beef shank or two chickens or a lot of soup. It's great for batch-cooking. A 15-quart stockpot, however, will get you through most of the recipes for this book. The most important thing is that the stockpot have straight sides and a tight-fitting lid and that it be optimized for your life. If you live in a tiny apartment, maybe this isn't for you. If you don't plan on making large quantities of food, maybe you just need a medium Dutch oven. Do what makes sense.

A SIZABLE RONDEAU

A rondeau, a flat-bottomed straight-sided pan, is a versatile shape. It can act as a soup pot or a stockpot and it's good for braising. You can shallow-fry and deep-fry in it if you want, but it's also shallow enough that you can sear—and flip—meat in it, flipping it easily.

A DUTCH OVEN, OR A WIDE HEAVY-BOTTOMED PAN WITH A LID

A Dutch oven is like a rondeau but deeper. It's perfect for things that are more brothy and that need to stay warm for longer. A Dutch oven also warms evenly on the sides. I have a 15-quart one that is a fairly lavish expenditure, but I think of it as an investment, since a well-treated Dutch oven is fairly indestructible.

TWO MIXING BOWLS, MAYBE THREE

You can get stainless steel mixing bowls for a fairly low price. It's better to have more of them than you think you'll need. (A large mixing bowl doubles as a rubbish bin, too, to store vegetable cuttings and garbage as you cook.) You'll definitely need two, since many recipes call for mixing together dry and wet ingredients separately and then combining.

A STAND MIXER

A stand mixer is not a necessity, but it is massively useful, especially if you have attachments like a meat grinder and a pasta sheeter. If you want to make a lot of desserts, or if you want to make freshly sheeted pasta, or if you ever want to grind your own meat (or make potato latkes), a stand mixer with these attachments will make your life easier. So no, you do not *need* a stand mixer. You don't need a car, either. You could survive with a horse and buggy, but something with a motor will get you there faster.

A NO-FRILLS FOOD PROCESSOR

I happen to like chopping vegetables. It's therapeutic for me. But if you don't—and if you have a lot of prep to do and little time—a food processor can be extremely useful. It does in 30 seconds what it takes 30 minutes to do by hand. Food processors—we always call them Robot Coupes in restaurants, even though that's just a brand—can cost thousands of dollars, but you can get a good one, without all the bells and whistles and many space-occupying attachments, for under a hundred. It can make mayos, salsas, chop veg for soffritto, dressings, etc.

A Few of My Favorite Things

Generally speaking, I'm not a big gadget guy. No chef I know is. The less you have to keep track of, the better. That said, after spending nearly three decades in a professional kitchen, a handful of tools have proven themselves if not necessary then greatly appreciated. They do a lot, take up little space, and save hours of your time. In a restaurant, that time is spent cooking more food. At home, it's spent with your loved ones, which makes these tools even more important for a home cook.

Y-PEELER

Most home cooks have a vegetable peeler that looks like a wand. The first day you step into any professional kitchen in America you're presented with a Y-peeler. Ergonomically it's the only thing that makes sense. It gives you much more control when contouring and with much more speed and efficiency. The one I've always used is by Kuhn Rikon. It's cheap as dirt and when, like every other peeler does, it craps out on you, you don't have to feel bad about throwing it in the bin and getting a fresh one.

MANDOLINE

A Japanese mandoline is a guaranteed time-saver. I've been using one for twenty something years. I've lost chunks of my palm, tips of my pinky, I've cut down to the bone on my thumb. But man, does it cut things paper-thin extremely fast.

SOME REALLY FUCKING SHARP KNIVES

You can do the majority of kitchen jobs with two knives: a 12-inch (30cm) chef's knife and a paring knife. A chef's knife, especially the 12-inch one, can handle larger jobs such as chopping or breaking down a chicken and take

the place of a slicer. Paring knives, which range in size from to 3 to 4 inches (7.5 to 10cm), are necessary for smaller more fiddly tasks like paring, obviously, or slicing garlic.

People are obsessed with Japanese knives, and as a cook in a restaurant I completely subscribe to that obsession. Japanese knives, made with Damascus steel, can be sharpened to an obscenely sharp edge. But as a dad at home, I think Japanese knives are frivolous (to maintain that edge, you need to constantly sharpen them). I prefer Swiss or German knives, which are made with a harder steel. Wüsthof or Henckels or Forschner (now called Victorinox since the companies merged) are all good knives at varying degrees of expense (Wüsthof is the most expensive, Henckels the least, Forschner in the middle). Get a set of Forschner with plastic handles for a good price, and honestly, they could last you forever. No matter what knives you purchase, learn to use a steel to keep the edges true. Or, find a local butcher, hardware store, or knife shop that sharpens knives. Do this every few months and your experience in the kitchen will be much more rewarding.

PEPPER MILL

Preground pepper is gross. Why? Peppercorns are berries and, as a berry, are full of essential oils and nuanced flavors that begin to degrade as soon as they are ground, especially when ground finely. With preground pepper, you end up with an overwhelming spice but no nuance. Freshly ground black pepper, on the other hand, can be full of fruity and earthy notes. It isn't just spicy but delicate, too. So, get a pepper mill. It can be a fancy wooden one or a cheap plastic single-use one. The quality of the grinder is less important than just grinding pepper to order.

SCOOPERS WITH SCRAPERS

An ice cream scoop with a metal band to release the mixture from the scoop—also called a disher—comes in handy beyond scooping ice cream. A uniform size means a uniform cooking time. Equal size is also important for inevitable arguments about fairness between siblings. Size is also an easier measure than using a scale. I use a #10 scooper, which is about 3 ounces (6 tablespoons), for things like forming meatballs, cookies, and pancakes. But I have a 1-ounce (2-tablespoon) and a 2-ounce (4-tablespoon) scoop on hand, too.

DIGITAL KITCHEN SCALE

You could go your whole life cooking normally without a digital scale. You could even be a pretty good baker, too. But if you are someone who has any desire to start baking in any kind of more ambitious capacity, a digital scale is going to be your best friend and most trusted companion. (Baking is a much more exact science than cooking, hence the reputation of pastry chefs as meticulous, introverted, and a little grumpy.) Even if you aren't going to become a master baker, get a digital scale. Grams are by far the most exact way to measure, which is why we've included grams in the book, and why

they're used by all restaurant chefs. A good scale won't cost more than $20.

METAL BENCH KNIFE

In the pastry department, a bench knife—also called a bench scraper or chopper—is used to cut and separate dough. But that is just the beginning of its superpowers. I keep a bench knife near my cutting board at all times. It's perfect for transferring ingredients from the board to a pot or a bowl. It's also great for cutting pasta shapes. And I use it to scrape any schmutz off my wooden table or cutting board, which is especially important when making dough.

PLASTIC BOWL SCRAPER

In any professional kitchen, you'll undoubtedly find a plastic bowl scraper, universally called a plastic card, in everyone's back pocket, kept there until the need arises, as it inevitably does, to scrape the last bit out of a deli container or a plastic bowl or if they need to pick up a mess of chives. It serves a similarly wide range of purposes at home.

METAL TONGS

I recommend you buy metal-tipped utility tongs from a restaurant supply store, IRL or online. Personally, I love the tongs from Vollrath. These tools are not for delicate food but are great at turning, transferring, and fishing elements out of a braise. They offer good grips at a distance, which is key to avoiding the often painful, and always messy, disaster when something splashes back into the pan.

HALF-SHEET PAN WITH WIRE RACK

You need one but I recommend three if you have the space. (They stack.) At 13 × 18 inches (33 × 46cm), they fit into most home ovens. (If they don't fit in yours, get a few quarter-sheet pans, which are 9½ × 13 inches/24 × 33cm.) The key here is the wire rack, which allows air to flow beneath whatever sits atop it. One of the biggest mistakes home cooks make is roasting meat on a flat metal surface, which cooks not only on one side but unevenly as well.

RICE COOKER

A rice cooker is a parent's best friend. Set the rice to cook, leave for 5 hours, come back, and you'll be greeted by perfectly cooked—and kept—rice. My favorite is a Zojirushi (it has a little elephant on it and sings you a little song when your rice is ready). Also, its "quick" setting is magical.

BAR KEEPERS FRIEND, BRILLO PAD, AND A GOOD BRUSH

If you've cleaned your dishes as you've cooked, hopefully by the end of the night you'll have only a few serving plates to clean. But sometimes life doesn't turn out like that. Sometimes an angry tower of dirty dishes awaits you like a bunch of hoodlums down a dark alley. A tube of Bar Keepers Friend, a Brillo pad, and a good brush are all the backup you need. Bar Keepers

Friend, a bleach-free cleansing powder, is powerful yet safe for stainless steel. A sprinkle on a dirty pot or pan will save you precious minutes. A Brillo pad—a soap-impregnated scouring pad—is clutch for stubborn *fond* and keeping your stainless steel spotless. And a good brush, stiff of bristle and sturdy of construction, will greatly expedite the final battle of the night.

How to Source Ingredients

I'm a professional chef, born and raised in the Bay Area. So I skew toward locally grown ingredients from the farmers' market, and local butcher shops. I'm also lucky enough to have a garden, for the first time in my life. I've even started hunting. But I understand this is not always the reality for everyone, whether it's because fresh ingredients are out of range geographically or financially. Unless I say that an element is 100 percent necessary for a recipe, feel free to make whatever changes you need to make. It's more important that you cook than that whatever you're making exactly aligns with what's in the book. That said, I am writing this cookbook from my perspective and I'm sharing my personal preferences, developed after years in the kitchen. So if you are able, what follows are some of my favorite staples.

OLIVE OIL

I use a lot of olive oil. More than seems reasonable or even advisable. But trust me, olive oil is the turbocharged engine of pleasure. That said, olive oil is not a level playing field. You can have fake olive oil; you can have rancid olive oil; you can have poorly made olive oil. On the other hand, you can have well-made, fresh, great olive oil. You can have esoteric, single-origin, estate-harvested olive oil that is so expensive you hardly know what to use it for. My advice is to find a trusted brand that is somewhat widely available. My go-to is Partanna, which is made from Nocellara del Belice olives from Castelvetrano in Sicily. It's both widely available and in the midrange in terms of price. But experiment for yourself. Some olive oils are fruity, some spicy, some grassy. In my house I usually have three or four open at a time. The other thing to keep in mind is that olive oil needs to be used. It's not something you want to hold onto for long.

SALT

I am a man of many salts. Some for seasoning things like soups or large batches of veggies or mashed potatoes; some for finishing. In the case of the former, I'm a Diamond Crystal kosher salt guy and all the measurements in the book use that. (Kosher salt is much less salty than iodized fine table salt, which is the only salt I *never* use.) For finishing salts, I have a stable of assorted salts, from grey French sea salt, to Maldon flaky salt, to Himalayan pink salt. Unlike olive oil, salt keeps, so get as many as space allows.

BUTTER

Not all butter is created equal. There's a lot of super-expensive butters that I like, but one that

I've been able to find everywhere is Kerrygold Irish butter, unsalted. I'm absolutely addicted to it. It's one of the most consistently delicious butters and I love the fact that it is grass-fed. If you can't find Kerrygold, look for a grass-fed butter with a golden or yellow color, which indicates higher fat content.

CALABRIAN CHILI BOMBA

To call Calabrian chili bomba a condiment is to vastly underplay its importance in the kitchen. A combination of fermented and pickled chiles with garlic confit and olive oil, bomba Calabrese (or bomba di Calabria) is never far from my reach. I use it on sautéed vegetables, in pasta, on fish and shellfish, in compound butter, as a marinade. I am biased, obviously, but I recommend Che Fico's own Calabrian Chili Bomba, available online on our website, but any good store-bought brand will work.

PASTA

I feel strongly about dried pasta. The brands I really like are De Cecco, for a high-quality mass-produced pasta; Gentile, for a super high-end product (a little hard to find); Rummo for a gluten-free pasta; and Rustichella d'Abruzzo, an artisanal producer from Abruzzo that uses heritage whole-grain wheat, pure Apennine spring water, and bronze dies, and slowly air-dries the pasta. I keep my pantry stocked with four or five bags of pastas: a spaghetti or two, a short shape (like a rigatoni or a casarecce), an orecchiette, and shells.

A Very Important Note to Dads

This is an afterword of sorts but not an afterthought at all. It's something I've had in mind as I've written this book. It's something I wish I had realized much sooner in my journey as a parent. Here it goes: It's okay to prioritize yourself sometimes; it's okay to tell people around you that you need help; it's okay to take care of yourself. You aren't being selfish to take time for yourself. You aren't being weak to access and express your feelings. Showing up for yourself is a way to show up for your family. If you keep it all in, you end up showing up as a Dad you don't recognize, full of stress, holding in years of unspoken and unresolved emotional issues. We want to show up for our families as the best version of ourselves. When you're exhausted, stressed out, and bottled up, that's impossible.

What taking care of yourself looks like obviously depends. You know yourself. For me, as an ADHD having, chest beating, intensity seeking, Alpha male, I have a certain amount of aggression at any given time. To pretend that I don't just isn't true. I needed to come to a place where I could accept that my aggression isn't bad. It can be used positively just as it can be used negatively. It just is. I found that I needed a physical outlet. For me, that happens to be Brazilian Jiujitsu. Training is therapeutic. It's a terrific outlet for frustration, hurt feelings, embarrassment, and anger. What you're left with is self-confidence, emotional balance, self-control, and patience. Your dopamine spikes and your cortisol goes way down. It's thrilling and humbling. In any given training session, you are both the hammer and the nail. I have been lucky to also cultivate incredible relationships with other dads who have given me so much encouragement and guidance.

I'm in therapy, too, which has helped me work through a lot of childhood experiences. But therapy is just one tool, though an important one. My experience as a man has been that I really need other men in my life to push me and guide me and to be able to rely on. Historically it has been more acceptable for women to gather to discuss their feelings but I find these peer-to-peer interactions are vital for me. Iron sharpens iron.

Summertime Bagel

A Better Grilled Cheese - 001

Homemade Cheeseburgers!

Roasted Pork Rib Rack

Pie Process

A Better Grilled Cheese - 002

Chicken Nuggets à la Baba Galina

David + Vanessa

Fresh Pasta Dough

pycakes

!!

Failed Recipe

Pancake Process

Meatball Hero

Dad + Helena - 001

Dad + Helena - 002

Dad + Helena - 003

LOVE

Chocolate Cake

HA!

Crew

s - 001

Focaccia Process - 003

Dad + Helena - 002

107_Nayf_9780593537527_fpo...

Dad + Helena

Focaccia Process - 006

A Better Grilled Cheese

ACKNOWLEDGMENTS

The best way to describe my family is to watch the scene from the movie *The Town* when Ben Affleck tells Jeremy Renner that he needs a favor. The only question Renner asks is "Whose car we taking?" They have been there at every turn through thick and thin. Our pack runs deep and I feel grateful for every aunt, uncle, and cousin that has had my back since the start (Leaka, Beebs, Marge, Erina, Miya, Emi, Noah, Nathanael, Eilina, Edik, Tanya, Nikolay, Pasha, Ida). My brother, Misha Nayfeld, who credits me with being his first client (from birth), has been my best friend and confidant through life, and now happens to be my manager. My mother, Mama Galina, has pulled me by the scruff of my neck through every challenging time, like the most tenacious mother wolf in the wild. Thanks, Mom, for always believing. To my father, Mark Nayfeld, for teaching me that you don't need to be a victim of your circumstance. He had every excuse to fail as a father but he succeeded with style. My fiancée, Vanessa, is the first woman I've ever wanted to ask to marry me. We have both learned about what the right kind of love feels like. She makes me feel like home. I love you. She and Niko have also been the inspiration for a lot of successful recipes and the guinea pigs for so many failed ones.

My team at all of the restaurants, including everyone from partners to porters, have been the reason for our continued success. I appreciate your hard work and dedication. Especially my chef team that allows me to be the father I want to be: Jazmine Fenton, Kevin Flagg, Gio Luciani, Riley Draa. My original chef de cuisine of Che Fico, who is now our Culinary Director for the group, has been a rock next to me since the beginning. He was the only reason I have been able to pull away and be a better dad. Thank you, Evan Allumbaugh. The directors and partners of our restaurants, Bryn Barone and Jason Alexander, for holding down your end and loving hospitality like I do. My business partner, Matt Brewer, has been my work wife (or husband), depends who you ask. He has also become my best friend and brother. He is my family.

Casey Rebecca Nunes has held this group together (sometimes with glue and popsicle sticks). She has kept us on task and organized. Thank you.

The men in my life that guide me, shape me, push me have been crucial to my growth as a man. My BJJ coaches Aaron Zaballos and Stevie Martin at Z Mata in Castro Valley have been so much more than coaches to me. They have been therapists, friends, and guides. To all the teammates at Z Mata, I appreciate all the training and laughs, but, most important, the text threads. My cousin Max Berkovich, Josh Meier, and Oscar Gaytan are the "other brothers" that keep me seeing straight and working hard. They are my blood and chosen family. They are my squad. My friend and sometimes trainer and sometimes student, Roop Sihota, and his wife, Sharn. Thanks for opening your home to me and being real friends.

To the whole Alamedaville crew, you have made me a part of a community and I love you and your children.

To Laurence Jossel and Holly Rhodes for your abject kindness and NSA love.

To Ben and Kelly Kovacs for opening your home to me during one of the toughest times of my life. You made it so much better.

To Joshua David Stein, you are great. You are better than you give yourself credit for. You are a beautiful man with a lot to offer. You have become a friend and a great collaborator.

To Eric Wolfinger, I'm so happy I got the full wolf. Your photography is stunning. You make me look the way I wish the world saw me.

To Andrea Lucich for your immeasurable wisdom and tricks up your sleeve with the photo shoots.

To Tom Pold, thanks for taking a chance on me. I won't let you down. To Michael Psaltis, thanks for always checking in and being a great book agent.

To my other Jewish moms, Susan Hosmer and Stephanie Davis, PR just doesn't cover it. You're my family. Thank you for sticking by us.

To my dear friend Lynda Marren, you are truly a champion of chefs. Our industry is better because of you.

Over twenty-five years of cooking I've been lucky to work with great chefs, cooks, and dining room personnel. Thank you to all of you who have helped shape my journey.

To Lee Wolen, the late Jamal James Kent, Bryce Shuman, Evan Funke, Chad Colby, and Adam Sobel, the few chef pals that I'm grateful to keep up with.

To Donna Gibbs and the rest of the attorneys at BGDO Family Law, you know what we've been through. Thank you.

To my cooking protégés Dick Costolo, Jared and Ronnie Middleman, and Bob Fisher, thank you for being friends and teaching me about things I never knew.

To Gwyneth Paltrow, who has had no reason to be nice to me besides just being a good person and a great friend. Also, she loves good food.

To my dog, Cassidy, in a strange way you got me ready to be a dad. You saw me through a lot. All the stuff you chewed up is forgiven.

Most of all to my daughter, Helena Nayfeld, without whom there would be no book and no one would have asked me "Dad, what's for dinner?"

—David Nayfeld

〰〰〰〰〰〰

The first time I met David, in Alameda, California, he made me go for a five-mile run. "I don't run," I said. "C'mon," he said, "it's normal." "But I don't have shoes," I protested. "Borrow mine," he replied. So, I did. We've been running ever since, David semi-patiently waiting for me as I struggle to catch up. After that first forced jog, David saw that I wouldn't quit and began to trust me. So, I thank him first and foremost for pushing me and for trusting me and for making me part of his family. I was in very good company. Also, sorry, David, but I'm never going to run again. (We can roll whenever you'd like!)

This book would not have been possible without the yeoman's work of Casey Rebecca Nunes, who was vital at every single step of this project. Thanks to Eric Wolfinger, long-haired lover of the lens, who makes everything idyllic, in life as in photos. Thanks to my agent, David Black, the nicest bulldog in the business. Thanks to Tom Pold, man of enormous chill and untold skill.

I'd like to thank my blood family, too. My mom, Marcia Lieberman, for letting me crash at her house on my trips to Alameda and for picking me up at SFO and for being my mom and making her applesauce meatloaf and creamed company tuna. She's not a very good cook but she's a *very* good mother. Thanks to my sister, Rebecca—and Eli, Noah, and Chris—for being a warm, supportive, and really just the best sister. Thanks to my sons, Auggie and Achilles, for too many things than there is space to list here.

—Joshua David Stein

INDEX

(Page references in *italics* refer to illustrations.)

broccolini:
    and Italian Sausage Lasagna, *112,*
      113–17, *115*
    Smothered Italian Sausage, *138,*
      139
    White Pie with Ricotta, Sausage
      and, 247–8
broth:
    Sipping, 39
    Stracciatella, 55
brown butter:
    Chocolate Chip Oatmeal Cookies,
      271–3, *272*
    Sauce, 118, 122
Brownies, Peanut Butter, 262–4, *263*
brush, for cleaning, 292
Brussels Sprouts, Creamy Shaved,
    with Bacon, *197,* 204
butter, 293
    Brown, Chocolate Chip Oatmeal
      Cookies, 271–3, *272*
    Brown, Sauce, 118, 122
butter beans:
    Lemony, *196,* 202–3, *203*
    Pasta e Fagioli, 81–2, *83*
buttercream frosting:
    Chocolate, *269,* 270
    Vanilla, *266,* 267
Buttermilk Cornbread, 259–61, *260*
Buttery Tomato Soup, 52–4, *53*

C
Caesar Dressing, 184–6
Caesar Salad, 184–7, *185, 186*
cakes:
    Chocolate, with Chocolate
      Buttercream Frosting, 268–70,
      269
    Cuppycakes with Vanilla
      Buttercream Frosting, 265–7,
      266
    Strawberry Rhubarb, 281–3, *282*
Calabrian chili bomba, 293
Carnitas, Pork, 168–9, *170–1*
carrots:
    Glazed, with Lime Juice and
      Butter, 218–19
    My So-Called Curry, 206–7
    Vegetable Minestrone, *59,* 60–1
cast-iron skillets, 288

cauliflower, in Chicken Enchilada
    Stew, 62–3
cavatelli, ricotta:
    Homemade, 105–9, *106–9*
    with Pork Sausage, 110, *111*
cheddar cheese:
    A Better Grilled Cheese, 226,
      227–9
    Biscuits with Sausage and Pepper
      Gravy, 28–31, *29*
    Shepherd's Pie, 175–6, *177*
cheese:
    A Better Grilled Cheese, 226,
      227–9
    Pie, 245–7
    and Spinach Ravioli, Handmade,
      118–22, *119–21*
    see also specific cheeses
Cheeseburgers!, Homemade, *164,*
    165–7, *167*
Che Fico! (San Francisco), 3
chef's knife, 290
chicken:
    breast, Red Wine Vinaigrette as
      marinade for, 189
    Caesar Dressing as condiment
      for, 184
    Enchilada Stew, 62–3
    Fried, "Jew-ish," 152–5, *153–5*
    Grilled, Pesto Sandos, 232–4,
      233, 234
    Grilled, Save Your Ass, 137
    handling safely, 155
    Milanese, 142–5, *143, 144*
    Miso Honey Mustard Baked,
      140–1
    Nuggets à la Baba Galina, 134–6,
      135, 136
    Soup, Jewish Mother's, 67–8, *69*
    Stock, 36–7
chickpeas:
    Chopped Salad with Red Wine
      Vinaigrette, 188–9
    My So-Called Curry, 206–7
Chili, Turkey, *64,* 65–6, *66*
Chili Spice Mix, 65–6
chocolate:
    Banana Walnut Bread, 256–8,
      257
    Buttercream Frosting, *269,* 270

    Cake with Chocolate Buttercream
      Frosting, 268–70, *269*
    Chip Oatmeal Brown Butter
      Cookies, 271–3, *272*
    Double Dark, Cookies, *272,*
      274–5, *275*
    Peanut Butter Brownies, 262–4,
      263
Chopped Salad with Red Wine
    Vinaigrette, 188–9
"clean as you go" adage, 7
cleaning, tools for, 292
coconut milk, in My So-Called
    Curry, 206–7
Collard Greens, Tangy, with Lemon
    and Chile Flakes, 194, *195*
conchiglie, in Pasta e Fagioli,
    81–2, *83*
cookies:
    Brown Butter Chocolate Chip
      Oatmeal, 271–3, *272*
    Double Dark Chocolate, *272,*
      274–5, *275*
cooking with your kids vs. cooking
    for your kids, 9–10
corn:
    and Green Beans, Creamy,
      196–7, 198–9, *199*
    shucking, 198
Cornbread, Buttermilk, 259–61,
    260
Cream, Spicy Rigatoni with Tomato,
    Roasted Peppers and, *84,* 85–6
cream cheese, in Summertime
    Bagel, *230,* 231
Creamy Corn and Green Beans,
    196–7, 198–9, *199*
Creamy Polenta, 220–1
Creamy Shaved Brussels Sprouts
    with Bacon, *197,* 204
Creamy Tomato Sauce, 46–7
Crispy Roasted Sweet-and-Sour
    Mushrooms, *197,* 211–12,
    213
Crispy Skin Pan-Roasted Salmon
    with Tomato Basil Relish,
    160–3, *161*
Croutons, Judy Rodgers's, 187
cucina povera, or "poor man's
    cuisine," 87